THE UNZIPPED GUIDES™
for everything you forgot to learn in school

Peterson's

Essays
UNZIPPED

C. J. Bennett

PETERSON'S

A **nelnet** COMPANY

PETERSON'S

A **nelnet** COMPANY

About Peterson's, a Nelnet company

Peterson's (www.petersons.com) is a leading provider of education information and advice, with books and online resources focusing on education search, test preparation, and financial aid. Its Web site offers searchable databases and interactive tools for contacting educational institutions, online practice tests and instruction, and planning tools for securing financial aid. Peterson's serves 110 million education consumers annually.

For more information, contact Peterson's, 2000 Lenox Drive, Lawrenceville, NJ 08648; 800-338-3282; or find us on the World Wide Web at: www.petersons.com/about.

ISBN-13: 978-0-7689-2488-6
ISBN-10: 0-7689-2488-X

Printed in the United States of America

10 9 8 7 6 5 4 3 2 1   09 08 07

First Edition

MORE UNZIPPED GUIDES

Newswriting Unzipped
Research Papers Unzipped
Short Stories Unzipped
Speeches & Presentations Unzipped

CONTENTS

INTRODUCTION

Can Writing an Essay
Be Easy?

I USED TO dream of being transformed into a genius—able to learn foreign languages after a single day in Spain or France. I couldn't walk by a piano without feeling drawn to the keys, imagining myself lowering my head and then miraculously finding all the right notes to a Chopin etude, maybe shifting to some jazz or rock and roll, and then ending with Beethoven—all this without ever having taken a single lesson. Does writing seem more mysterious than speaking several languages or playing the piano? If writing seems mysterious, it's because people—especially writers—love to romanticize it. This book does the opposite. It de-romanticizes writing.

A magician makes things appear, pulls the ace of spades or an egg from behind your ear, and it doesn't make sense, and you shouldn't believe your eyes, but the trick is clever. You smile and applaud. There are tricks to writing. Most books forget that a trick should be quick. When the magician reaches behind your ear, he'd better not linger. When a writer is willing to confess his tricks, he should get right to the point.

What is my point? This book—even if you just browse one chapter—can help transform your writing, save you time, and boost your grade. If you are reading this book, it's because you want something fast. You may already be thinking about skipping ahead. No problem. I've got lots of tricks that can help you write that essay. Each trick is pulled from the chapters that follow and you will find more tricks in each chapter. This is a book of tricks. I want to give you enough tricks so that you'll get top grades in all your classes. You name the subject. You name the essay.

You may already have a writing manual, but this book:

- Gives you just enough "trickery" without burdening you with long and tedious detail

- Gives you some insider knowledge, such as how some teachers can get fooled into giving you a higher grade

Here are your first twelve tricks. You may know some of them, but I bet you don't know all of them. There are more tricks to come. This is *Essays Unzipped.*

1. The essay assignment does not necessarily use the same language found in the syllabus, such as specific phrasing for the course title, description, or goals. Make use of terms and phrases found in the syllabus. These phrases can help you connect the specific essay assignment with the larger concerns of the course, and this strategy will win you points.

2. Question: How many types of essays are there? Answer: More than a million. Nevertheless, you can divide essay assignments into two types: 1) persuasive and 2) descriptive. Even the descriptive essay needs to persuade the reader that it has something to

offer. Revised answer: There is only one type of essay. It is the persuasive essay.

3. Set a timer and free write for 20 minutes. Do not take your fingers off the keyboard. If you get stuck, use the following prompt: "I feel stuck because . . ."

4. Create an interesting title by selecting a poetic quote from your readings. Follow it with a more descriptive subtitle: *"Transformed into a Genius: How the Unzipped Book Saved My Life"* or *"A Trick Should Be Quick: Analysis of the Unzipped Book."*

5. Simplify your thesis. If you have three parts to the thesis, ask what the common denominator is. Isolate the three phrases and then free write how each phrase connects to the larger controlling idea. Try to recast the thesis as having one overarching argument or theme.

6. Create tension by thinking about your larger theme (violence, mall culture, a difficult poem) in relationship to its opposite. Introduce violence by considering what it means to be safe, introduce mall culture by thinking about primitive bartering societies, think of the difficult poem in relationship to a very accessible poem. Set up the opposite, make the connection to your real subject, and allow the tension between the two subjects to introduce your thesis.

7. Never use the word "conclusion" in your conclusion. It sounds as if you need to tell your reader what should be obvious through the content of your concluding paragraph.

8. Most writers do not spend enough time commenting on their insights. As you fill your paragraphs with insights, analytical claims, anecdotes, illustrations, and other material, comment on how and why this material is important to your argument or analysis. Use phrases like "this is particularly important" and "this helps to explain."

9. Essays written for exams need to err on the side of over-emphasizing everything. The exam essay will rarely be read with the same care as a "normal" essay, so you should consider dividing the essay into sections and using subheads to create extra emphasis for each section.

10. The fastest way to build a strong bibliography is to examine and evaluate the bibliographies of published writers before finding your own list of essential texts.

11. Start revising by simply printing the essay and looking at how the words and the paragraphs appear as objects on the page. Initially resist reading a single word; instead simply look. You will start to

find formatting errors, such as missing indents, strange paragraphing, lack of italics for titles, and strange block quotes.

12. Create a document of your success. Photocopy positive comments from past papers, creating an inspirational collage. Feel free to add an extra A+ or two. Is this too corny for you? Jim Carrey, long before becoming the star of hit movies like *The Mask* and *Ace Ventura*, wrote himself a check for millions of dollars, essentially creating a document to help him visualize success. Why not create a mechanism for visualizing your own college success?

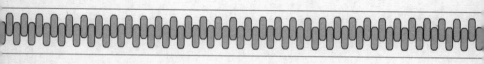

CHAPTER 1

Tease, Test, or Trap:
Figuring Out the Assignment

IS GRADING SUBJECTIVE?

Students and teachers are often distrustful of one another. Distrustful students believe teachers "give out" the good grades to their favorites. Fueling this belief is the subjective nature of grading. Did I just confess that grading IS subjective?

Most writing manuals will not discuss this sensitive issue because they are written by educators who must defend their grading standards and processes. I am willing to confess that there is some element of subjectivity to grading, but don't fool yourself. Some students abandon any hope of improving their skills (and their grades) because they believe subjectivity and favoritism determine everything. They do not. Studies show that essays receive similar, if not identical, grades from different graders.

WHY YOU NEED TO READ THIS, ESPECIALLY IF YOU THINK THAT YOU DON'T

Teachers provide a number of different resources to guide students or to answer the question: "What do I want?" Students, on the other hand, state that they have read the assignment carefully but sense there should be more information, more guidance, more something.

How hard can it be to follow an assignment? I have heard teachers complain for years that students don't listen and don't read. Many students continue to trap themselves in past performances—perhaps learned in high school. "What do you want?" distrustful students ask. "Look at the assignment," the teacher responds.

I believe there is one serious impediment to students understanding what is asked of them. While most college assignments ask students to PRODUCE knowledge, most high school assignments ask them to REPRODUCE knowledge or simply reiterate what they have read or been told. Don't be trapped in a high school mentality. It is really not that difficult to be original.

On to the tricks . . .

ANALYZING THE ASSIGNMENT

Some essay assignments provide descriptions of problems or examples of areas of analysis. You want to begin by separating the claims from the questions.

Does the Assignment Allow Much Room to Explore?

Some assignments supply a specific question while others ask several questions. How do you find focus? Make sure you understand what is being asked. Does the assignment require the exploration of several problems or questions (linking the parts of the assignment with "and") or does it provide options (linking these options with "or")?

Does the Assignment Invite You to Provide Depth Rather Than Breadth?

Most weak essays race over several questions, topics, and texts. Real estate agents have a mantra: location, location, location. Your mantra should be: focus, focus, focus. Let the specifications of the assignment guide your focus, but also recognize that you'll need to address development and depth.

Should You Ask Questions About the Assignment?

Most teachers welcome discussions about the project. Even if you think you understand the assignment, think of discussing it with your professor as a way to begin building your approach or as an opportunity to clarify your understanding of key terms and unformed ideas. Most teachers will begin viewing you as one of their serious students for simply asking these questions. Don't be shy; be rewarded.

GET TO WORK: EXAMPLE OF ANALYZING AN ASSIGNMENT

The Sample Assignment

> *Claudia Koontz's* Mothers in the Fatherland *argues that women were far from innocent bystanders during the rise of the Third Reich. Although Alison Owings's* Frauen: German Women Recall the Third Reich *may serve similar purposes, the history presented in this book comes from the many interviews of various women (guards, persons of mixed heritage, a countess). Although Koontz's book may be argued to be the more polemical work, how might Owings's collection be seen as a polemic?*

The Analysis

This assignment comes in three sentences. Like many assignments, this one begins with a claim. It is not a highly debatable claim and it should not be interpreted as the assignment. It's the "set up." Increasingly, professors ask students to position one text against another because this makes plagiarism difficult. In the second sentence, the assignment is starting to look like a compare/contrast paper, but the third sentence clarifies the focus: "How might Owings's collection be seen as a polemic?"

What Is the Assignment?

It is important for students to understand that professors often construct assignments that search for complexity and so parts of the assignment may seem open to interpretation. If I were handed an assignment like this one, I would ask the professor to clarify whether the essay should focus strictly on the Owings book or on both books. If I was unable to get a fast answer, I would use Koontz's book to set up my analysis of the Owings book. I would highlight my interpretation of the assignment by using much of the language of the assignment.

Analyzing the Assignment in Relationship to the Rest of the Syllabus

How does the assignment relate to the course goals or description? Most professors supply a description of the course at the beginning of the syllabus, often indicating some of the class goals. Consider how the essay assignment relates to course goals or the course description. Sometimes these goals provide a wonderful way of framing your project. Listen closely to course terms and concepts. Incorporate them right into your paper.

Don't Be a Copycat

Sometimes before an assignment is due, teachers will actually model how they want you to execute the assignment. Pay particular attention to these classes, but beware! The teacher is modeling how to analyze the text not providing the analysis for you to simply reproduce. Class lectures should be viewed as a resource not as a crutch. If you do make use of class discussions or lectures, understand and indicate how your essay moves beyond this material. Remember, it is essential that you PRODUCE and not simply REPRODUCE.

GET TO WORK: DISTINGUISHING YOUR CONTRIBUTION

If the professor has already discussed the first interview in Owings's anthology, do not write an essay on that well-covered material. Instead, you might mention this first interview as an opportunity to look at a very different aspect of Owings's anthology. Try the following:

> *"Although the first interview in Owings's* Frauen *may be considered exemplary of narration built upon detail, many of the subsequent interviews invite examination of the vague accounts and the indirection that suggest a very different type of narrator."*

Notice how this fine introductory claim begins with the teacher's claim but then subordinates it with the student's own contribution. This will win big points. There is no easier way to highlight an essay's commitment to *producing* than by building upon what already exists. You may think of this structure as typified by the following sentence pattern: Although we already know X, no one has yet explored Y.

ZIP TIPS
Grading Rubrics

Professors are increasingly providing grading rubrics, which may look like a spreadsheet of characteristics of the essay—everything from "Clear Thesis" to "Developed Paragraphs." Most students do not enjoy reading these documents and they are not always identical. Don't get fixated on this document, but use it to help you understand, for example, specific concerns of your professor, such as a particularly weighted concern for research or an unusual emphasis on terminology.

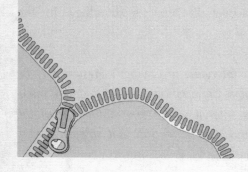

HOW TO HANDLE ASSIGNMENTS WITH A LARGE SCOPE

When the scope of the assignment seems very large (e.g., examine a major historical event or explore a diffuse social dynamic), think of ways to focus attention. For example, if you are asked to analyze a presidential autobiography, you might focus on the most personal passages—the accounts of family and friends—as a way of exploring a contrasting tone. Remember: In exploring the personal part, it is easy to demonstrate how the more focused and manageable parts help you to understand the whole. In other words, you are still examining the entire book but through the lens of this one specific concept: the personal passages.

HOW TO HANDLE ASSIGNMENTS WITH A SMALL SCOPE

When the scope of the assignment seems very small (i.e., consider the way a presidential autobiography addresses the personal life), think of ways to connect these "marginal" concerns to the larger thrust of the book. For example, in his autobiography, *My Life,* how does Bill Clinton represent his relationship with his wife? Consider how your analysis of this specific aspect of his autobiography relates to Clinton's larger effort to "connect" with readers and perhaps emphasizes the relationship between the larger concern and the specific analysis in his introduction and conclusion. In fact, the relationship between a narrow analysis and a larger concern is a classic way to argue the importance of a focused assignment.

QUICK TIPS

- Rewrite the assignment in your own words. Ask yourself how it is different. Do you understand the key terms? Now rewrite the assignment but add terms found in the course description or terms used during class discussion or lecture. Make sure you understand those terms.

- What would your essay look like if it had a more narrow focus? Consider providing a closer focus on key aspects of the text, the question, or the topic. Recognize that this focus can still encompass much about the broader examination of text, question, or topic as long as you make the connection for your reader.

- Cut the parts of the assignment apart. Tape them near your workspace. Do the same with key phrases from the course description and/or course goals. Think about the relationship between these various terms and phrases.

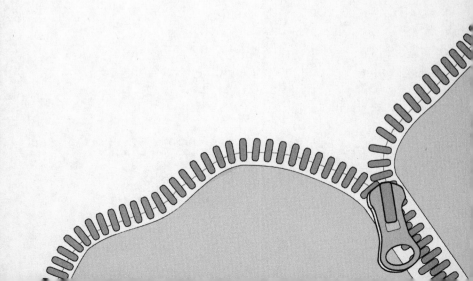

CHAPTER 2

Which Essay Should You Write?

HOW MANY DIFFERENT TYPES OF ESSAYS ARE THERE?

Your professors, depending on their fields of study, label their assignments as position papers, descriptive essays, analytical papers, research papers, and a host of other names. To make matters worse, your teachers probably assume you understand the difference, even though they may not realize that other teachers in other disciplines have other names for the same paper. A position paper for your anthropology professor may look identical to the response paper required by your philosophy professor and an analytical paper for your political science professor might be renamed as a compare/contrast paper by your English professor. Does this sound confusing? Let's make it simple.

There is really only one type of *essay:* the persuasive essay. But I would suggest that there are two types of *assignments:* "descriptive," which hides the fact that it requires some sort of persuasion, and "analysis and argument," which clearly requires persuasion.

It is tempting to categorize essays as informative or persuasive, descriptive or argumentative, but there is a danger in these categorizations. Don't be fooled into believing that your professor only wants a description of your summer vacation. Think of the "artful" Personal Statement you wrote to persuade the admission committee that you deserved admission to their college. Everything you write should serve to persuade your teacher to give you an A+.

Every piece of writing must reach, impress, and even convince the reader of its worth. So how do the many names for essays both clarify the assignment and confuse students? It is important to recognize that these categories overlap and there are no simple or ideal types. Let's begin with the deceptively "simple" descriptive essay assignment.

ESSAY ASSIGNMENT ONE: DESCRIPTIVE

How to Recognize It

This essay may seem like the easiest to write. You may find your professor asking you to write this "basic" essay early in the semester. Your teacher may think of it as a "testing the water" essay, an opportunity to see if you can construct a coherent sentence (not

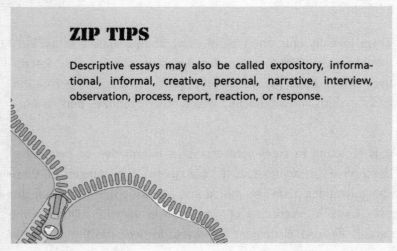

ZIP TIPS

Descriptive essays may also be called expository, informational, informal, creative, personal, narrative, interview, observation, process, report, reaction, or response.

to mention a coherent essay). For classes in the social sciences (psychology, history, political science, sociology), your teacher may ask you to describe your personal thoughts on ethnicity or democracy or you may be asked to interview someone in the medical profession or someone in your family. In philosophy, gender studies, English, or education, you may be asked to describe an experience or state an opinion about some subject.

This assignment may invite you to simply convey your observations of a text, a person, or an event, but the persuasive potential of this type of essay is always implicit. Even if your professor can truthfully claim to expect no "persuasion," your prose will persuade, hopefully, that you *are* in command of the subject. Everything is persuasion and the sooner you recognize that, the better off you will be.

ZIP TIPS

Easier Said Than Done

More than any other assignment type, this one will be examined closely for its form. Although teachers often think of this assignment as a "gift" because it is not as saddled with the demands of analysis, argument, or research, the descriptive essay is one of the hardest to write.

How to Write It

Life is full of ironies. For example, it is ironic that the descriptive essay, which seems to ask for so little (certainly not as much as the analytical essay), is really the most difficult. Beware the crazy complexity found in simplicity—but find the complex, ironic, paradoxical possibilities. Your professors will delight in your interest in life's ironies.

Almost every topic lends itself to explorations of irony. If, for example, you are asked to write about the best thing that happened to you over the summer, consider something that seemed less than wonderful but that also provided a lesson or led to something wonderful. If you are asked to describe mall culture, use it as an opportunity to consider how mall culture is most powerfully observed not in the central walkways or even in the stores but in the parking lots or at closing time. Find that surprising moment when the culture of the mall is most rich with contradiction as it moves from business to silence. In searching for contradictions, you are discovering complexity. This helps distinguish your descriptive essay from the tedious narratives that simply describe, without concern for irony, paradox, contradiction, complexity, surprise.

ESSAY ASSIGNMENT TWO: ANALYSIS AND ARGUMENT

How to Recognize It

Although it's best to think of all essays as persuasive, some essay *assignments* call for analysis and argument, which are fundamentally about persuasion. Let's look at these two common terms: analysis and argument.

What Is Analysis?

Analysis considers how things work. How do the parts relate to the whole? This is a basic question that might be used to begin your analysis. When you ask questions about birth order, you might begin to analyze what it means to be the baby of the family. We can consider a specific aspect of birth order and then generalize about it in relationship to the general topic. For example, it is interesting to recognize that some people are the youngest members of a family for many years before another child is born—at which point everything shifts. If a psychology professor or sociology professor asked you to analyze your position in your family, you might move beyond a description of your family (a specific example) to an analysis that takes into account psychological or sociological principles (general principles), such as Freud's

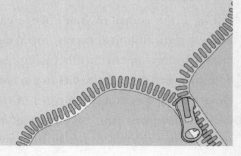

ZIP TIPS

Analysis and argument essays may also be called compare/contrast, cause and effect, classification, thesis/support, interpretation, literary, explication de texte, close reading, review, inquiry, exploratory, deductive, or proposal.

concept of the Id, Ego, and Superego or Lacan's notion of the Real and the Symbolic. Although your professor will undoubtedly supply most, if not all, of the key concepts, he or she will probably expect you to do some independent thinking about how those concepts might be used to analyze your family or some other target subject.

What Is Argument?

There are implicit and explicit arguments. The quality of your prose makes an implicit argument that you are knowledgeable, articulate, and professional, but for most assignments your professors will expect more than quality prose. You will be expected to have an *explicit* argument, serving some point, such as analysis.

So what is the difference between analysis and argument? As stated earlier, they overlap. Analysis is by its very nature argumentative. Many essay assignments invite you to argue for your point of analysis. Don't, however, make your reader work too hard to see the argument in the analysis.

How to Write It

Just as in the course of your college career you will be asked to analyze texts, historical events, social dynamics, economic trends, current events, and many other things, so, too, should you analyze your own writing process. Get in the habit of analyzing everything (your teacher's syllabus, the types of courses you are required to take, the layout of your campus) and you will become a first-rate scholar. Here are two examples to analyze.

Example from a Weak English Essay

Toni Morrison's Beloved *has been read as a ghost story, a slave narrative, and a family drama. It is certainly all these things. It is also a historical text, though it is a work of fiction. This essay examines* Beloved *as a work of history.*

MORE TO UNZIP

Three Classic Steps to Building the Argument

We could analyze the revised example further to say that it is built upon three classic steps:

1. Set up what other people believe or have stated.

2. Suggest an alternative reading.

3. Indicate how you plan to develop that alternative reading.

Revised Example That Emphasizes the Argument in the Analysis

Toni Morrison's Beloved *has been read as a ghost story, a slave narrative, and a family drama. It is certainly all these things, but it is essential to keep in mind that it is also a historical text. Scholars have observed that Morrison took the basic details of her story from the account of Margaret Garner, who killed her daughter rather than allow her to be sent back into slavery, but these scholars often emphasize that Morrison quickly moved from fact to fiction. This essay argues that* Beloved *always reminds us that it aspires to the historical. In each of its three sections,* Beloved *highlights its function as historical document, one that offers a view into slavery like no other.*

The first example certainly points to analysis and it highlights what it will examine. The thesis, however, is rather vague and the reader isn't sure that there is a real argument. The second example retains the same focus, but it works to emphasize its argument. It even states *"this essay argues . . ."* It also indicates that the unusual argument, which certainly is debatable (and that is good!), will examine (i.e., analyze) how the three sections of the novel "highlight" the novel's function as history.

QUICK TIPS

- If the assignment is presented as a question, try to restate it as a statement. This statement, which might include a claim and a stated reason, may serve as your thesis statement.

- If the assignment describes a task, how might you form it into a question or a series of questions? These questions (or question) may serve to generate ideas for your argument. Most writing manuals steer you away from forming your thesis as a question, but creating a list of questions is a classic way to generate ideas. Use it. In fact, you could begin every assignment by writing twelve questions that respond to the assignment prompt.

- Talk about the assignment. Talk to the professor in or out of class. Talk to fellow students. Make sure your ideas are very different from their ideas. Talk to anybody who will listen. The more you talk about the assignment the better it will go.

- Do not announce the type of essay (i.e., position paper or analysis) in the title of your essay. Transform the title "An Analysis of Toni Morrison's *Beloved*" into "History Announces Itself in Toni Morrison's *Beloved*" and transform "An Interview with a Recent Immigrant" into "Immigration Anxiety in the Words of Anchee Wong." Note how the transformed titles eliminate words like "analysis" and "interview."

CHAPTER 3

Starting in the Middle and Ending at the Beginning

STOP BEGINNING AT the beginning. Everything goes faster when you start in the middle. Introductions require too much thought. Don't begin at the beginning!

Almost everyone agrees: the introduction should be written after you have written the body of your essay. All the experts beg students to hold off on writing the introduction until the end, but still everyone ignores this advice. Why? Most students are afraid that they have nothing to say or they worry that if they start writing without a clear direction, they may go off topic and have to delete pages. Don't worry. Just write.

DON'T OVERTHINK IT

Stop overthinking. Is "overthinking" a word? Don't worry about it! You need words; you need pages. If you spend time overthinking, you will never generate enough pages or enough ideas.

Go to the library and watch how quickly people type e-mail responses to friends. Go to the movies and watch couples and groups of kids discussing what they just saw. Start a rumor at school and notice how quickly everyone jumps into the discussion. We are word machines. You are a word machine. If I could step inside your brain, how many thoughts would I find jumping from one place to another? Don't overthink. Write.

E. M. Forster offers this advice: "How do I know what I think until I see what I say?" Forster is suggesting that thinking is not enough. To generate ideas, perhaps to even grab hold of them before they dissipate, you need to speak or write down the ideas. Feel free to articulate your argument to a friend or to the mirror, but don't kid yourself. If you just speak the ideas silently in your mind (if you just think the ideas), you will get nowhere fast. Students always cheat themselves by remaining silent. Get your ideas out there. Write them down.

Writing, for most people, is painful. People don't want to waste any time creating extra words until they know exactly where they are going or what exactly they will say. Fear of writing, therefore, keeps people from writing. Fear of not having enough pages keeps students from having enough pages. Yet students will think nothing of writing thousands of words when they e-mail friends and family, even though those words evaporate into the Internet. Write the body of your essay as if you are writing an e-mail to a friend. You might even begin like this:

> *Dear Jennifer, I have to write this terrible paper about Toni Morrison's hard-to-read novel* Beloved. *I kept thinking, "Why doesn't she just write a history book?" In fact, I would rather read a history book, even though her novel does let us see things that no history book would ever let us see.*

Notice how the ideas in this stream-of-consciousness e-mail are not that different from the Morrison example presented in the last chapter. In writing an e-mail about the assignment (even if you write the e-mail to yourself), you may find something to write about and begin to discover your argument.

GETTING UNZIPPED

When you feel as if there is nothing left to write, ask yourself why you think there is nothing left to write.

For instance:

> *I don't think analyzing my response to the terrorist attack on the World Trade Center is very interesting because I was very young when it happened. I would rather interview my grandmother, who was in Manhattan at the time. She always said that I was too young to understand what happened. She always said that it wasn't just about the loss of the people or the loss of the buildings but the loss of security. Maybe if I talk about my conversations with my grandmother I am still talking about my response to the terrorist attack because my grandmother's words of wisdom are part of the event, at least in my experience. Could I write this paper about my responses to my grandmother's stories?*

So, in this example, the very problem of being stuck ends up yielding new material. We simply need to ask, "Why am I stuck?" The answer may lead to interesting ideas.

Three Tricks for Free-Writing

1. Set a timer for 10 minutes.

2. Do not lift your fingers from the keyboard; just think of this as a 10-minute finger exercise.

3. Do not allow yourself to use the backspace key; just keep typing. Do not stop writing until the timer rings.

Three Tricks for Cheaters

1. Place the timer on the other side of the room.

2. Turn off your monitor so that there is a dark screen and you cannot see the words forming into sentences. You could also tape paper over the screen. There is no looking back. Go forward.

3. If you hit a mental block, start typing the following sentence and finish it: "I think I am blocked because . . ."

One Cheater's Trick for the Good Writer Who Never Cheats

Good writers, those students who have actually learned something about sentence structure or paragraphing or the beauty of word choice, will need to turn off their internal editor. Because you are such a fine writer, you may need help interrupting that editor in you. It is easier to free write (really freely think) when you are free to write sloppily, suppressing the editor and letting the creative genius through.

> *Don't allow yourself to use any punctuation and just keep writing and dont stop even at the end of a sentence certainly not to place a period there but instead keep writing and use lots of ands and just keep writing and you will begin to loosen up because you will recognize that the final product does not need to look pretty.*

VISUAL LEARNERS AND IDEA MAPPING

If free-writing allows a rush of ideas to be generated, an idea map can help give shape to those ideas. Tap into a childlike spirit of play, while creating some seriously astounding and brilliant results, with this three-step strategy:

1. Place the main topic in a circle in the center of the page.

2. Draw radiating lines from that central idea and begin brainstorming related ideas, images, and phrases. Be free. Allow every thought to find its way onto the page. In fact, try to encourage yourself to place wild thoughts first, ones that seem especially unrelated. These wilder thoughts will often generate the most interesting material.

3. Examine the relationship between the central idea and the other ideas. Can you start to see hierarchies?

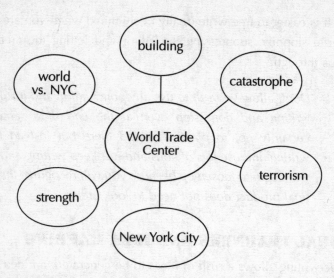

Take a second topic and make that the center of another idea map. If we take "catastrophe," we might then generate the following:

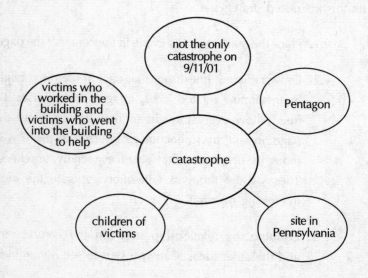

Take a third topic and make another idea map. If we take "victims" then we might generate the following:

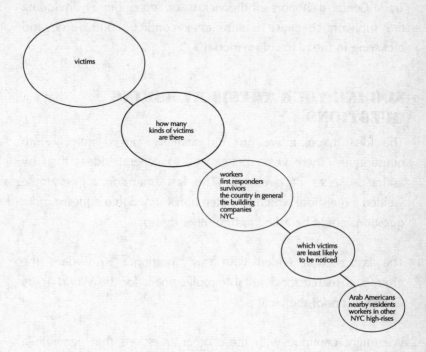

- What must it be like for surviving victims to endure the prolonged process of deciding what to erect on the site?

- What is the irony here? Prolonged indecision results from instantaneous and decisive catastrophe.

- Can I write an essay on this single irony? How does the protracted search for a suitable replacement for the World Trade Center dishonor the victims?

Our idea maps have produced a thesis for an essay that will argue that the protracted search for a suitable replacement for the World Trade Center dishonors all the victims of September 11, including the survivors, because it substitutes conflict, controversy, and bickering in the place of memorial.

FINDING YOUR THESIS BY ASKING QUESTIONS

The idea mapping we just did actually moved quickly into questioning. There is no better way to generate ideas than by asking a series of questions. The last brainstorming example yielded a question, which was then transformed into a thesis; more questions could be asked to find other theses.

The last section ended with this question: "How does the protracted search for a suitable replacement for the World Trade Center dishonor the victims?"

We might continue with these other questions that generate a potentially better thesis:

- Who is most affected by the bickering over the World Trade Center site?

- What has been erected at the other sites and how is the World Trade Center site different?

- Has this debate served to keep the pain of 9/11 alive?

- Is the controversy over the site actually helpful in allowing people to have something to help them process their loss? Give them something to direct their energies—and even their anger—to?

- Can I write this paper and stay sensitive to the very real losses of people who are much closer to the event than I am?

FIVE CRAZY PROMPTS TO GET YOU ASKING MORE QUESTIONS

You should ask any and all questions. Just as in the first two brainstorming strategies, this one invites you to freely write everything down. Don't criticize. There will plenty of time to critique later. To help you think about ways to push your questions into new areas, consider the following:

1. How can one question invert another question, actually turn it on its head—or ask the completely opposite question?

2. How can I generate other questions by replacing one point of view with another or by replacing one large aspect of the topic with a much smaller (or detailed) aspect?

3. Why is this question interesting to me? Would other people (my parents, my teacher, or a person of

another race, ethnicity, gender, class, sexual orientation, religion, or nationality) ask a very different kind of question?

4. What happens when I think of the kinds of questions people from another century would ask? What surprising details would I have to first explain? What background information would they need to know first?

5. What is the most outrageous or taboo question? How might that be reshaped to yield a more responsible question?

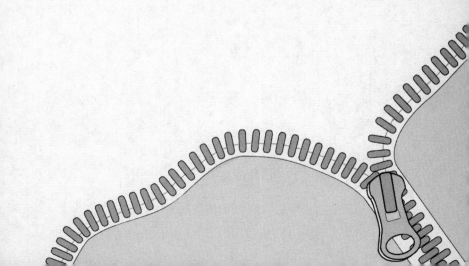

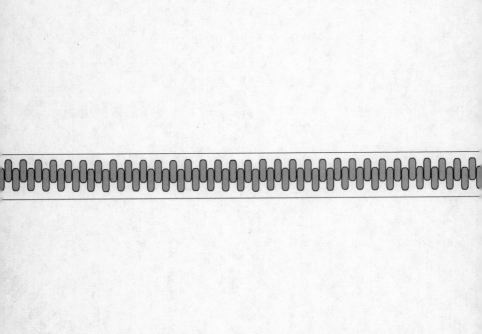

CHAPTER 4

Why Do the Little Things Mean So Much?

AN ARTFUL INTRODUCTION can convince your teacher to read everything that follows with great kindness and can make your bedazzled professor forgive any problems in the body of your essay. You know the expression "the clothes make the man," and although it is terrible to think that surface counts for so much, it does. Have you ever met someone and formed an opinion about him or her right away? Studies actually show that we all do this. Reading an introduction is like meeting someone for the first time. We may not want to make a quick judgment, but we do. Even before teachers read the title, they form opinions about the general look of the paper. Is it smudged, crinkled, or ripped? Is there a colorful paperclip in the corner or—worse—an unprofessional fold where there should be a paper clip or staple? What would Donald Trump say about this? "You're fired!" Don't give your teacher (or Donald Trump) the chance to dismiss your work or you.

THE FORM

Many professors ask you to present your work in a certain form, sometimes specifying font size and even where to place your name, the date, and other details. Before you turn in any paper, examine the syllabus for these guidelines. If the teacher does not indicate a form, place the following information at the upper left side of the paper:

- Your name

- Course title and number

- Date

- Word count

Skip two lines and type the title of your essay, which remains in the same font and without quotation marks or italics. Center this title. Single space the title if there is more than one line.

There are two common errors that can mark your paper as unprofessional:

1. Playing with the title, i.e., putting it in bold, italics, quotation marks, or, worse, altering the font size or color

2. Printing problems, resulting in a difficult-to-read document or messy or faded copy

No professional writer would submit a faded or messy document. Would you?

THE TITLE

The title is as much an introduction as anything else. I have heard professors praise a student's title as if the title were the entire essay. Unfortunately, students spend much more time creating clever names for e-mail or MySpace. When my students turn in their papers, I often take a few minutes to read their titles in class.

Students respond to the strong and interesting titles and hear what a difference a good title can make. I never again have to tell them to get creative with their titles because they understand and want to create a title that will make their classmates gasp—as if they have just seen someone doing flips.

Tricks for Finding an Interesting or Professional Title

Many professional journal papers make use of a two-part title, the subtitle separated from the main title by a colon. You might think of the main title as the hook and the subtitle as the explanation. Most students write very direct titles, like "Analysis of Toni Morrison's *Beloved*" or "A Study of the World Trade Center Disaster." Let's imagine ways to write a hook, one that shows your creativity, one that will win you points. Let's imagine these two titles as being more mysterious, more poetic, or more captivating.

Boring Titles

Analysis of Toni Morrison's Beloved

A Study of the World Trade Center Disaster

Transformed Titles

Beloved History: An Analysis of Toni Morrison's Beloved

Trading Stories: A Study of the World Trade Center Disaster

The original titles, which are too direct, lack magic. In our transformed titles, the direct, or explanatory, title gets moved into the subtitle position. Playing with words found in the subtitle allows us to create a new main title. "World Trade Center" inspires the phrase "Trading Stories" and the title of Morrison's novel gets redeployed as an adjective for "History." In addition, the word play of the new main title implies what the essay will be about and is meant to capture the reader. The essay for the Morrison novel examines history, specifically the novel's "love" of history and the essay on the World Trade Center explores the relationship between a grandmother's stories about 9/11 and the student's own stories. "Trading Stories" suggests the topic, yet keeps some mystery.

Titles from Quotations

Disremembered and Unaccounted For: An Analysis of Toni Morrison's Beloved

Reflecting Absence: A Study of the World Trade Center Disaster

History Is a Voice: A Study of the World Trade Center Disaster

In these examples, the original titles, once again, have been moved to subtitles, but this time the main titles have been created from quotations. The first quotation comes from Toni Morrison's novel and relates—in a poetic way—to the topic of history. Novels lend themselves to supplying beautiful quotations, but you would be surprised how often a poetic phrase can be found elsewhere. To find a quotation for an essay about the World Trade Center (which, after all, is not a text as much as it is an event), I first searched the Internet and found a quote from the Lower Manhattan Development Corporation, which has a Web site that commemorates the World Trade Center. "Reflecting Absence" seems perfect for the imagined essay; you may or may not choose to cite your source for the quote. (We are not in the area of plagiarism because you cannot copyright a title.) I found my second quote ("History Is a Voice") by searching online for quotations that have to do with telling stories. Get creative. You'll know the perfect quotation when you see it.

EPIGRAPHS

An epigraph (not to be confused with an epitaph) goes between your title and your essay. It suggests to the reader that:

- You have so much writing that it is spilling over.

- You can make interesting connections between the quotation and your topic; in other words, you are proving your ability to think beyond the perimeters of the assignment.

- You think like a professional, not a student, and are aware of the form for the epigraph.

Students love including an epigraph because

- it adds length to a paper;

- it is a fast way to get started;

- it is an easy way to distinguish a paper on the very first page.

Where to Find Your Epigraph

In addition to the very quick solution of searching online quotation resources, look for epigraphs in:

- classroom materials and textbooks

- newspapers or current magazines and journals

- books, lectures, Web sites, and theorists mentioned by your professor

ZIP TIPS

An Epigraph That Gets Double Use

Sometimes people use an epigraph and then open the introduction with a reference to it. "This quote from James A. Froude may help explain . . ." Although there are advantages to double using the epigraph, the single use creates the biggest surprise and suggests that you can make interesting connections.

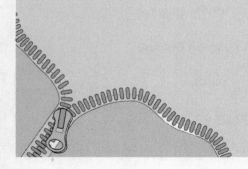

Can Anything Be Made into an Epigraph?

If you decide to select something from current events, make sure it doesn't dumb-down your topic. When in doubt, a quotation from a philosopher, world leader, or inventor will associate you and your essay with greatness in a way that quoting a pop singer, comedian, or famous crook will not. There are, of course, exceptions and you may want to risk a little irony, especially if the play between a serious title and a playful epigraph makes the irony clear—

Freud and the Family: Making Sense of Birth Order

"There is no such thing as 'fun for the whole family.'"
Jerry Seinfeld

FIVE TRICKS FOR ADDING LENGTH WITHOUT CONVEYING WEAKNESS OR A LACK OF MATERIAL

1. An epigraph not only adds a line or two to the very opening, but there also needs to be space above and below it. The epigraph should be single-spaced to set it off from the double-spaced essay, but it still adds length.

2. Do you have short paragraphs? Are there more than two or three paragraphs to the page? There is no set length, but take a closer look at those paragraphs. Add reflection to each paragraph, using sentences like the following: "This is important in order to

understand . . . " or "Most people will not at first see
. . . " or "A wonderful example of this can be
found in . . ."

3. Find an image, chart, or graph or create your own
visual to insert into your paper. Be sure to make
great use of the image. Get creative, but make sure
to comment on the added image. In an essay on the
World Trade Center called "Trading Stories," which
examines a grandmother's first-person experience in
relationship to the author's secondhand experience,
it would be useful (and it would take up room!) to

ZIP TIPS

Deceptions Far Worse Than Having a Short Paper

- Teachers recognize when you have played with the margins, font size, or spacing. Don't do it.

- Everyone knows that quotations can provide length. Don't overuse them.

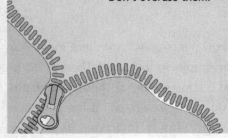

include a visual image of the attack on the World Trade Center. The essay should then comment specifically on the image.

4. Consider making a block quote from a short passage, even a single line. Do this when you want to bring special attention to a particularly strong quotation.

5. Professional publications in almost every discipline make use of "Notes." These provide an interesting way to include more information that may seem like a digression if included in the body of the essay, but which is useful and professional as an endnote or footnote. Your notes may provide further reflection on a topic or references to other articles and what you think of them. Notes might explore other related information that could not be worked into the body of the essay, further distinguishing the range of your intellect.

HOW TO QUOTE LIKE THE PROFESSIONALS

If you learn how to quote like the professionals, you will distinguish your work from all the other students who handle quotes awkwardly in their papers. The Modern Language Association (MLA) style will probably serve you best. Information about various conventions, citation, and research is also readily available on the Web. Here is what I tell my students.

- When quoting, show your ability to be selective and even economical. Don't, for example, always provide the entire sentence, but instead trim the quote down to its most important phrase and slide from your words "to the essential words."

- Some disciplines use an ellipsis (those three dots) to indicate missing material from a quote, but most only use the ellipsis in the middle of a series of words and not at the beginning or end.

- Quotes need to be introduced. Use the full name or just the last name of the author to introduce a quote, informing your reader that, for example, John Mulrooney argues that "life began in Edgemore Gardens."

- Because quotes need to be introduced, it is awkward to begin a paragraph (especially the first paragraph of the essay) with a quote.

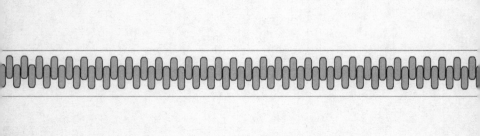

CHAPTER 5

The Thesis:
It Can Make or Break You

IS THE THESIS REALLY THE MOST IMPORTANT PART OF THE PAPER?

Every teacher, every writing manual, and even most students will agree that the thesis is the most important part of the paper. So why do students continue to get into trouble? Let's begin with three myths.

Myth #1: Everyone should develop a strong thesis before they start writing.

Reality: The thesis, like every aspect of the essay, should be a work in progress. Feel free to have a provisional thesis early on, but recognize that you may find the real thesis only after free-writing, brainstorming, or even completing the body of the essay. Rather than thinking of the thesis as coming before or after the other stages, think of the thesis as being examined all along the way. It is far more difficult and time consuming to adjust the body of your essay (the nuts and bolts of the argument) to an outmoded thesis than to simply revise your thesis. Feel free to find a thesis early but think of it as a flexible guide, one that can be adapted to new findings and developing arguments.

Myth #2: If my professor's assignment asks a question or invites me to argue a point, I don't need to read this chapter about developing a thesis because there is nothing left to do but answer the question or argue the point.

Reality: Many (if not most) college assignments guide students toward a specific thesis, but you don't want to write exactly the same paper as everyone else. Your teacher may provide a question, but a question is not yet a thesis. Even an invitation to argue a point or position still needs to be shaped into a tight and unique thesis. Most assignments invite the smart student to be creative and shape the thesis further.

Myth #3: My thesis should include the three parts of my argument.

Reality: There may be times when this three-part "signpost" makes sense, but it is often more effective—especially in short papers—to just include your overarching argument. It is often unnecessary (and a bit formulaic) to list three claims or three reasons or three points. When in doubt, simplify your thesis. The complexity should come from the argument itself and not from the announcement of the three parts of the essay.

HOW TO COME UP WITH A THESIS

There are many brainstorming strategies for finding an interesting topic for a dynamic thesis. Don't lock into a thesis too quickly. In fact, it is useful to think of the thesis in the early stages as a hypothesis or even a simple idea.

Thinking Inductively Versus Thinking Deductively

Remember "inductive" and "deductive" from your science class? Surprise! Your humanities essay assignment can use these two strategies for approaching a topic or argument. If you were asked to analyze a poem (we'll use Morris Harper's "Love Animal"), you might set out to prove that the poem uses metaphors to create a subtext of anxiety. You have a hypothesis, maybe one that follows a strategy demonstrated by the teacher, but you begin to work deductively, exploring the parts of the poem (the metaphors) to prove that the poem offers a subtext of anxiety. This deductive strategy will probably lead you to "discover" the most obvious things about the

MORE TO UNZIP

Love Animal

—Morris Harper
(reprinted with permission)

Love flew into the room,
Dropping feathers along the way,
Not bothering to find

The traps carefully placed
On the floor and chest of drawers.
A day later, love swarmed

And doubled, frantic
To be living such a short life,
To die before reaching

Some unknown scent.
It took three days to clean
The mess. Then

Came a third
Visitor through the door,
Sat in a chair, spoke

A few words ("May I have
Tea?"), and backed into a pillow
to wait for one simple thing.

poem. If you were to work inductively, however, you would start without the theory to be proven, working without a clear view of the outcome. You might simply start by noticing that the poem has a lot of metaphors. You would then gather them together, describe them, and perhaps even categorize them into groups. After asking several questions of the metaphors, you might observe that the first four metaphors associate love with animals or animal behavior, while the last two associate love with humans and human behavior. You begin to see a pattern and develop a thesis that states: "Morris Harper's 'Love Animal' uses metaphors to argue that true love can be characterized, ironically, not as a feature of animals but something distinguished from the animal in us."

Questions

Almost everyone agrees that the best way to find a thesis is to ask questions, such as "Why has reality TV become so popular?" (cause and effect) or "Should there be helmet laws?" (evaluation) or "Are Target ads more sophisticated than K-Mart ads?" (analysis through comparison). In working through these questions, you will eventually make a claim, such as "Reality TV has become increasingly popular in an age of fractured families and disconnected communities." Move, in other words, from question to claim.

Can you include the original question in the essay? Some published essays do feature stated questions, and logic argues that these questions lead to claims. Think of questions as especially useful in generating ideas and leading to a clear thesis. Although they should not be viewed as substitutes for a thesis, they can certainly create energy and clarity in your essay.

Idea Mapping

You can idea map by yourself *and* with others. Surprised that mapping can be a group effort? Let's look at a collaborative exercise in mapping. I frequently have students work in pairs or even in a large circle where the idea map circulates around the room. Although idea mapping works fantastically as an exercise that frees one person to create and gather his or her thoughts, idea mapping can also be built upon external prompts. This exercise is meant to unzip you from the everyday thoughts. Let's start.

Draw a circle in the center of a piece of paper and in that circle write a short phrase. Without giving yourself time to think, write responses to the following ten questions:

1. What is its opposite?

2. What is an example of its opposite?

3. What is a cliché that makes you think of the main topic?

4. Where is the tension or complexity in the main topic?

5. What is the most volatile or controversial aspect of the topic?

6. What is a movie, TV show, or song that relates to the topic?

7. What is a theme or topic that seems unrelated to the topic?

8. How is that theme really related to the topic?

9. What are the dangers of writing about this topic?

10. How might you introduce this topic to someone from the year 1800 or 2150?

If I were to create a quick idea map for the topic "The Attack on the World Trade Center" I might find some of the above questions and prompts easy and some impossible. The impossible questions often yield the surprising results. Here are some answers to the prompts above, which end with the tenth prompt moving into free-writing:

1. Safety of the Empire State Building

2. A house that is being erected rather than destroyed

3. The day the world changed

4. Maybe this was not the day the world changed

5. Was the U.S. at all responsible

6. *Apocalypse Now*

7. Dance

8. Dance is beautiful; destruction is not. Dance is expressive; destruction is expressive.

9. Will people be offended by my analysis/argument

10. For people in 2150, I might free write this response:

    We believe the entire future will look back at September 11, 2001 and recognize it as the day the world changed. I am afraid to hear your answer because it is important that I think that this day changed everything. I'm not sure why I believe it is so important, but I now believe I have an essay topic. I want to answer this question: "Why is it so important for me to believe the world, not just the U.S., fundamentally changed after September 11, 2001?"

ADDING EXTRA FOCUS AND SURPRISE TO THE TOPIC

Many papers are difficult to write because they are so easy to write. Let me explain. Most students stop when they find the topic that seems familiar and easy. When asked to write an essay about violence on television, they all write that it is bad. When asked to debate whether gay marriage should be allowed, they construct arguments for or against gay marriage, often choosing a position they believe will echo their professor's values. Isn't there another, less predictable, way into a topic?

Find a better focus. Don't be fooled. Most essay assignments still provide ample room for you to add focus and surprise, and this is one of the easiest ways to distinguish your work. I would even argue that the more proscriptive the written assignment seems, the more important it is for you to find your distinguishing focus. Let's look at our two examples.

Example of How to Refocus the Topic of "Violence on Television"

How can the topic of violence on television surprise us? Won't every student be writing the same paper, some version of:

Violence on television is bad.

Violence on television isn't as harmful as everyone thinks it is.

At first, it seems that there will not be a lot of room to distinguish yourself.

What if we ask what "violence" means? Does verbal abuse count? Do dehumanizing representations of certain classes of people count? Or, rather than types of violence, consider ways of defining violence: Are all depictions of violence the same? What about depictions of violence that are stylized versus those that are gory? What about depictions that are glorified versus those that are seen as signs of evil? What about violence that is suggested (i.e., the off-screen depictions, such as when you hear the gun shot but you don't see the victim hit)? Are you nervous that your professor will feel that you have stretched the topic? Most professors love these focusing gestures. They recognize that the topic has not changed—it has only found depth.

Example of How to Refocus the Topic of "Gay Marriage"

This topic may feel like a logical debate that invites a pro or con position, but I believe these types of essay assignments (considering social-cultural issues) invite students to find creative ways into familiar debates. In other words, it is as if you have gone for an

MORE TO UNZIP

The Five "S" Checklist for Evaluating Your Thesis

- **Sentence:** You should be able to write your thesis in one sentence. If the thesis sentence is one of the longest and most complex sentences in your essay, it is time to simplify, clarify, and reexamine your claim.

- **Stand:** Make sure the thesis takes a stand and does not straddle two positions.

- **Scope:** Examine the scope of your topic. Focus it. The general thesis that "television violence results in many antisocial behavior," should at least begin to focus on a specific type of television violence or a specific type of resulting antisocial behavior. Brainstorm and tighten your thesis.

- **Significance:** If it is difficult to imagine any rational person being convinced by your argument, then you need to rethink your thesis.

- **Signpost:** Be sure the thesis clearly indicates where the essay is going. Read it to friends and then ask them to predict what the essay will discuss.

audition for a musical and you've suddenly discovered that the other 20 competitors are singing the same song. Quick, change your tune!

Brainstorm ways to add new focus and surprise. Why not shift the argument to media representations of the debate? Analyze the generational differences and argue why this generational difference exists. If the assignment feels more proscriptive (for example, if the assignment reads: "Write an essay that argues for or against gay marriage."), consider building your argument specifically on constitutional grounds or focus solely on economics or familial structures and relationships.

INVERTING THE THESIS

There is more than one way to stand something on its head. As you search for ways to make your thesis unique, consider inverting the thesis. An essay on birth order, for example, may find surprising new ways into the topic by inverting the focus to ask questions not about the child's but the parent's birth order: How, for example, does it affect parenting style? The essay on Toni Morrison's use of history in *Beloved* may invert the topic to consider not the history that *Beloved* references, but the history of other novels to which Morrison's book may allude. An essay on the World Trade Center may invert the question of how people "trade stories" of this event to how images get traded. Play with the thesis and let that play lead you to surprising ways of refocusing.

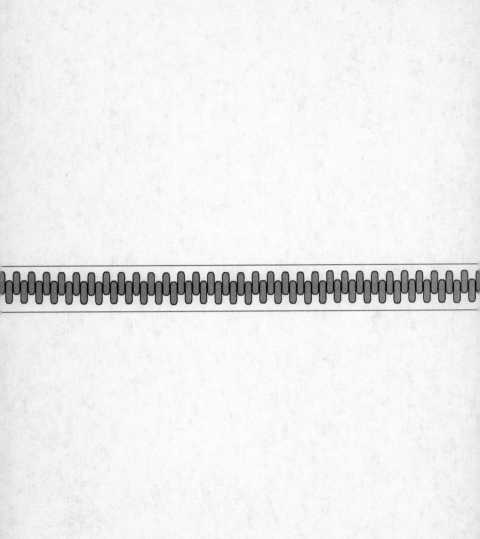

CHAPTER 6

The Funnel Introduction and Other Ways In

FUNNELING IN

Most students have been taught to build their introductions so that they move from a broad topic (the wide part of the funnel) to a narrow topic (the tiny spout of the funnel). You might also think about this formula as an opportunity to provide context for your topic.

Some succeed in writing beautiful openings and others fail. Students who are asked to write essays on gay marriage might think a natural context for gay marriage is simply marriage or gay rights. Students asked to write about violence on television may recklessly begin writing about television or violence in general. There is no faster way to convince your teacher that you have nothing to say.

Don't write the same essay that everyone else is writing, and please don't ruin everything by building an introduction that finds context in the broadest terms. Students, in their rush to get something on the page, will write first lines like the following: "Marriage has been part of American culture for many years." Or, "Americans witness a lot of violence. Violence is everywhere around us." If I were grading just these first sentences, these insipid generalities would receive failing grades. If I were interviewing someone for a job, I'd walk him right to the door.

Let's try working through this.

Weak and General Funnel Opening

Violence is everywhere around us.

Modest Change

When people most feel the need to relax, violence—transmitted through their television screens—haunts them.

This is still rather general, but it has a stronger verb and more complex sentence structure to disguise its weakness.

Radical Change

Children can now watch themselves depicted as the victims of violence at nearly any hour of the day, on almost every television station.

In this example, the topic of television violence gets added focus and surprise by narrowing the topic to depictions of violence toward children.

Radical Change with the Fiction Writer's Trick

Little Jason, with his first pair of glasses balanced on his small nose, and Sophie, who has just begun to sit up, can now watch themselves depicted as the victims of violence at nearly any hour of the day, on almost every television station.

The fiction writer transforms the generality (children) to representative children. The effect, which is powerful and visual, creates the

70   www.petersons.com

perfect hook for an opening line. In this sentence, you could also substitute detailed images for "depicted as the victims" or "nearly any hour," but I would not recommend loading the sentence with too much detail. The idea is to provide just enough to engage the senses of the reader without detracting from the general issues raised.

OTHER WAYS IN

The funnel opening offers a logical structure, one that begins by placing the topic into some broader context and funnels it from wide to narrow. Here are some other ways of providing context, continuing to use our television violence essay assignment for our examples.

Statistics

> According to the American Psychiatric Association (APA): "By age 18, a U.S. youth will have seen 16,000 simulated murders and 200,000 acts of violence."

It is easier than ever to find statistics for any paper—even nonresearch papers. You have no excuse.

Rhetorical Questions

> Why should you care about violence if you have never been a victim? Why should you care about depictions of violence on television if you don't watch violent shows?

Rhetorical questions tend to be overused, but they are an easy way to introduce the topic. At their best, they can be quite powerful. At their worst, simplistic.

Hypothetical Questions

Can the threat of violence be considered violence? Taken at its most extreme, imagine gunshots not to the body but inches away from the body. Is this violence? How about a threat to push someone off a five-story building?

For this particular subject, the hypothetical questions seem to work. You will note that these hypothetical questions raise issues of definition.

Definition

When most people think of violence, they imagine a fist, a knife, a gun, but not a word.

Notice how this definition does not insult the reader by providing a simple dictionary definition. Many students have been taught to begin with a definition, but a basic dictionary definition can actually make the essay seem childish.

Personal Anecdote

When I was 5, I saw a mother drag her daughter by the hair down the aisle of a grocery store, the young girl kicking and screaming as the mother shouted the most hateful words at her.

Some assignments invite this type of introduction, such as an assignment that asks students to consider their personal reactions to television violence or even an assignment that asks students to consider the "state of American culture." If you cannot tell by the assignment whether the personal anecdote is appropriate, ask your professor.

News, History, Fact

> *On a warm summer night in Texas, James Byrd was dragged behind a truck until he died. One of his sadistic executioners had an image of a black man hanging from a tree tattooed into his skin, a constant reminder to him of the long history of whites terrorizing blacks. While awaiting trial, the three murderers expressed pride in their crime. How did violence become such a way of life for these men? What moved them from racism and hatred to violence? Most Americans consume a steady diet of violence every time they turn on the television screen.*

Choose any topic and there are countless news stories, historical events, and facts that may serve to introduce your topic.

Review of Research

> *Martin Gruk's "Viewing Violence" argues that we are "raising a generation of monsters who know nothing but violence," and Sheila Traster echoes these cautionary words by stating that "the situation is so serious it is a national emergency."*

This review of research is a feature of a research paper or the professional papers written by your professors, but if you use just one reference to open a nonresearch paper you will certainly impress your professor. It is also a great solution to the problem of creating context without being too general.

Startling Claim (Direct)

Television makes fights.

Many writing manuals suggest this kind of opening and it is certainly effective. I do like the startling claim to come in a pithy, power-packed sentence.

Startling Claim (Metaphor for the Claim)

Every time parents sit their children in front of the television, they push them further off the cliff of safety and civility.

This opening sentence is not very different from the thesis ("Television makes children violent and parents need to take responsibility for that."). This introduction, however, not only disguises the similarity but also provides a specific and visual image of the thesis.

Other Tricks from Fiction Writers

The introduction can really be one of the most creative sections of the essay. Feel free to use hyperbole (*I witnessed a monstrous mother, fangs bared, dragging her daughter by a few strands of* hair.) or use metaphor. (*I witnessed a mother dragging a tornado of hair, glasses, and curse words down the aisle of the grocery store.*) Think of using specific examples rather than generic terms so that "Why should you care about violence if you have never been a victim?" becomes "Why should you care about muggings, domestic violence, or drive-by shootings if you've never even seen anyone lift a fist to another human being?" or "Why should you care about the smashing fist when you have only seen an open palm?" These efforts to transform language distinguish your work.

THREE TOP FAILINGS OF INTRODUCTIONS

1. Thesis is vague, unclear, or lacking argument

2. Extremely general opening

3. Too short

What if you can't find enough to say in the introduction? Several of the strategies we just covered provide easy ways to start your introduction. If you find that you still have only one or two sentences, you might ask whether you have fully developed the opening or whether the fault lies in your thesis.

Introduction with Vague Claims and Faulty Thesis

More people watch television now than ever and violence, which can be found on almost every station and at almost any hour of the day, is a part of our lives. (too general) There are, of course, effects of this daily consumption of violence. (vague claim) Perhaps the greatest damaging effect involves our youth. (vague claim) Television violence is creating a generation of aggressive youth. (vague claim)

Introduction with Focused Claim but Few Words to Actually Introduce the Surprising Thesis

Teenagers watch more violence on television than ever before. Studies show that this causes aggressive behavior in teens. American Idol, not often thought of as violent programming, also has deleterious effects on our youth.

Introduction with Focused Claim and Stronger Set-Up

Every time parents sit their children in front of the television, they push them further off the cliff of safety and civility. It is not, however, simply a question of violent programming. In fact, this concern for "violence" on television too often lacks nuanced debate about the very definition of the term. Although South Park provides one easy example of what people would call "violent programming," American Idol will seem an unlikely example. This popular television show, part of the explosion of reality TV shows, typifies the invisible violence of our era. American Idol dramatizes not simply winning, but weekly examples of failure and loss, and the center of this drama is not Paula Abdul, Randy Jackson, or Ryan Seacrest. It is Simon Cowell, the show's bad guy, who provides the conflict, serving up weekly doses of verbal abuse. The harsh and frequently heartless abuse, which in the press and in the populace gets both vilified and also surprisingly praised as honest, provides a violent undercurrent to the "celebration" of voice. American Idol *disguises its violent premise, but the undercurrent of violence is no less harmful to our youth and it deserves to be classified as violent programming.*

ONE MORE THING

I purposely chose a thesis that clearly takes a stand, one that requires the writer to argue and imagine many resisting readers who must be won over. The thesis is in its classic spot, the last sentence in the introduction, and this makes sense for a short essay.

Leading up to the thesis are eight sentences that might be characterized in the following manner:

1. A startling claim

2. Another way of viewing that claim

3. Statement of a problem with definitions

4. Two different examples of violent programming

5. Claim about the main subject, *American Idol*

6. Description of the show

7. Example of the show's violence

8. Claim that contrasts popular perception with the essay's version of reality

9. Thesis written in one simple sentence and clearly open to debate

The effort to win over resisting readers requires a writer to work toward introducing the topic without rushing it. Ease into your topic. Give readers a chance to get comfortable with the key terms and issues before you offer your surprising and debatable thesis.

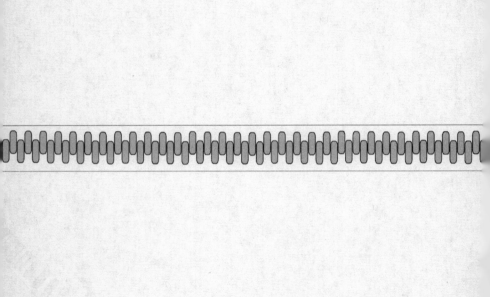

CHAPTER 7

Giving Body to the Body
of the Paragraph

THREE WAYS TO EXAMINE A PARAGRAPH

Students recognize when a paragraph lacks depth or detail, but they have difficulty fixing the problem. Rather than examining three parts of the sentence, such as the beginning, middle, and end, I advise you to examine the three aspects of the paragraph:

1. Topic sentence

2. Detail

3. Significance

The first two items in need of examination will seem familiar to you, while the attention to "significance" may be exactly what you've been missing. Once you learn to check for significance, you will discover new ways to create depth.

Topic Sentence

Your topic sentence serves to introduce the direction of the paragraph. Think of it as a(n):

- Billboard

- Signpost

- Announcement of a new subject

- Mini-thesis for the paragraph

- Defense of a new turn in the essay

- Encompassing claim about the materials that follow

- Topic with a controlling idea that makes a claim or further delineates the topic

- Rhetorical question that announces a shift in the essay

- Comparison that links the previous topic to the new one

- Statement of fact

Are Topic Sentences Necessary?

There are, in fact, countless examples of professional and powerful essays that do not slavishly structure their paragraphs upon the topic sentence. Will your professor notice if you do not begin a paragraph with a topic sentence? Maybe, maybe not. It is more accurate to say that your professor will recognize the effective use of topic sentences. It will make your essay feel organized. Topic sentences are particularly important for analysis and argument and less important to narrative and description. Get in the habit of writing topic sentences, but don't feel restricted by them.

Adding Details to Your Paragraphs

You may know instinctively what goes into a paragraph, but the following lists may encourage you to consider other possibilities. Be careful, however, not to simply build a paragraph by mindlessly adding details.

Illustrations or examples in the form of:

- Personal anecdote

- Historical fact

- Contemporary news

- Invented stories (from movies, novels, television)

Evidence in the form of:

- Personal experience

- Statistics

- Interviews (either conducted by you or from publications)

- Surveys

- Authoritative experts

Support, reasons, analysis, or explanations in the form of:

- Definitions, classifications, and analogies

- Cause and effect, compare/contrast, process

- Evaluation, critique, observation

Ask:

- Have I introduced complex ideas too quickly and would my paragraph benefit from further explanation?

- Is the topic sentence overburdened? Should I begin with a simple claim before following with a statement that highlights the complexity?

- If a sentence is particularly unwieldy, would it be helpful to divide it into two sentences?

- Would it be helpful to provide my reader with any of the following?

  o definition

  o statistic

  o anecdote

  o expert opinion

  o news story

  o historical fact

  o example

- If I have included an anecdote or a statistic, have I provided enough information about the source (the who, what, where of it)?

- Have I conveyed to my reader the significance of my information?

Adding Significance Is the Best Way to Add Depth to Your Paragraphs

You should ask this question repeatedly: "Why is it so important for me to provide this information and why am I pursuing this analysis?" After every new statement, perhaps after every new sentence, ask yourself, "Why should I include this and why does my reader need to know this information?" In answering these and the following questions, you will be providing significance to your essay's analysis or argument. (If there is a key phrase that helps to inform your analysis or argument, feel free to use that phrase several times. Think of your analysis or argument as being in a conversation with a professional critic (or critics). Any dialogue between 2 people yields a shared vocabulary and so, too, should your analysis or argument.) As an extra bonus, you will also be adding length and depth to the essay. This "body building" is far easier and faster than any other strategy for adding length to an otherwise short paper.

- Why is this information important?

- Why should my reader care?

- Why might some people overlook the importance of this information?

- Who might be especially affected or moved by this information?

- How does this information advance knowledge or understanding?

- Why am I placing this information in this section of the essay?

- What are the dangers of ignoring this information?

- How does this sentence advance my argument or analysis?

- What might a resisting reader say about my claims or information?

PARAGRAPH BODY-BUILDING

Let's examine what standard pieces usually wind up in the undeveloped paragraph, then what it looks like as writers begin to add material, and finally what it looks like when writers consider the significance of their various claims and statements.

The Thin Paragraph

The thin paragraph usually already holds the topic (the controlling idea) and a few details about that controlling idea. See, even this explanation is thin . . .

The Thin to Moderately Developed Paragraph

Students usually remember they can fill a paragraph with quotes, statistics, examples, and facts. Sometimes writers feel comfortable providing first-person anecdotes or hypothetical narratives. Some assignments invite compare/contrast, cause and effect, assertions and support. These assignments guide students to including certain original analysis or at least observations.

The Well-Developed Paragraph

The most startling feature of the well-developed paragraph, the feature that students rarely think to use, is the reflection on the controlling idea and the examples. These reflective statements may respond to a host of questions, such as:

- Why is this example useful?

- Why should people care?

- What is the significance of this topic?

- Why does this statement effectively counter the opposition or the resisting reader?

- Why is a certain point especially effective in addressing larger concerns of the paragraph or the essay?

How to Help a Thin Paragraph in Search of Significance

Inject a little personality into your essay by using the following words or phrases:

- Especially significant

- Perhaps most startling

- This powerfully explains

- The most shocking example

- The best illustration of this

- Perhaps nowhere else can we see

- Exactly

- Interestingly

- Uncannily

- Most

- Best

- Finally

I think you get the point that these words and phrases do not simply provide accents that highlight one part of your argument over another. They also provide personality, energy, and significance. The essay should not seem a constant stream of equally important ideas. One good idea after another begins to feel like a list, rather than like a developed argument. The essay, in order to feel rich with energy and passion, must create emphasis and convey some personality.

Students often ask me if they can make a personal address. I say the judicious use of the first person can be powerful. Not all professors feel this way. You will find no consensus on this question. Use the first-person address ("I") at your own risk or ask your professors whether they allow it or not. Don't, however, think that this is the only way to show your personality. A well-placed superlative ("the most important aspect" or "the best illustration of this") can make all the difference in the world in transforming an essay into something that feels personally engaged and powerfully presented.

Example of a Thin Paragraph

Oliver Stone's World Trade Center *is clearly a religious movie. There is a scene where Will Jimeno, played by Michael Pena, sees Jesus. Although movies frequently show death and may even depict it as a journey through a tunnel, the filmmaker chooses to specifically render a recognizable image of Christ. It takes no more than a few moments, but later Will talks about it to his sergeant. He makes his beliefs clear, and so does the film.*

Example of a Paragraph with Added Significance

Oliver Stone's World Trade Center *is clearly a religious movie. (controlling idea and topic sentence)* **The significance of this religiosity serves to raise interesting questions about the film's missing subject: the al-Qaeda martyrs who flew the planes into the buildings. (significance of the controlling idea)** *There is a scene where Will Jimeno, played by Michael Pena, sees Jesus. (example) Although movies frequently show death and may even depict it as a journey through a tunnel, the filmmaker chooses to specifically render a recognizable image of Christ. (description of scene compared to what other movies depict)* **This is a particularly dramatic moment in the movie. Death, or near death, is always dramatic, but**

> **this scene specifically dramatizes a very specific type of religious experience. (significance is emphasized)** It takes no more than a few moments, but later Will talks about it to his sergeant. **(detail) This discussion serves to emphasize what Will has gone through, reinforcing the event with an interpretation of the religious experience. (significance and explanation)** Will makes his beliefs clear, and so does the film. **(concluding point)**

After grading thousands of student papers, I know that most paragraphs are too thin. I am talking about a failure to include essential information that helps to develop a point. In addition to applying the strategies outlined in this chapter, take a first draft of your paper and write the following questions next to every paragraph: "Why should I believe you?" and "Why should I care?" Read the essay out loud. Read it out loud a second time, staying mindful of these questions, which are representative of your resisting reader. The resisting reader can be your best friend, keeping you honest and encouraging you to fully explain your ideas and the significance of each paragraph.

PARAGRAPH MYTHS

Myth: A paragraph should be comprised of four or five sentences.

Reality: Students love a clearly defined formula, but you should really resist this one. Paragraphs should not be reduced to measurement or counts. Logic suggests some ideas need more explanation than others and so the idea of allowing only a certain number of sentences for each paragraph does more than force art to function (or malfunction) as science. It seduces you into making illogical choices about when to finish a paragraph, effectively dooming your organization to failure.

Myth: A paragraph should have more than one sentence.

Reality: Writers have been known to create extra emphasis with a single-sentence paragraph. Although the single-sentence paragraph is mainly featured in certain kinds of writing, such as fiction, news, and magazine writing, it may also serve as a transitional paragraph in your essay. The exam essay, which requires a quick conveyance of information, may even feature a single-sentence thesis paragraph. The rules—as that very famous adage states—are meant to be broken.

Myth: The five-paragraph essay is golden.

Reality: All three of these myths address formulas based on counting. The five-paragraph essay, in fact, leaves no room for variation. The formula demands five and not six or four paragraphs. In following this formula, writers stop listening to the organic needs of the essay and make artificial decisions about paragraph length, development of argument, details to include, and support to offer. In addition, if I read a stack of papers and every essay follows the five-paragraph essay, the work begins to look sadly alike. Break free from this formula and distinguish yourself as an independent thinker and not a robot writer.

CHAPTER 8

How to Score
Last-Minute Points

A PASSION FOR ENDINGS

Can a weak conclusion lower your paper's grade? Don't take that risk. Can a great conclusion save you? Maybe. Your teacher may give you the benefit of the doubt for an awkward essay, one that may have skipped a few steps or offered thin support, if the conclusion is impressive. What makes an impressive conclusion? Well, it certainly isn't stale repetition. Most college essays are short and don't need to summarize three points or reiterate three aspects of the analysis or argument.

"But I was taught to summarize at the end," I can almost hear you cry to me. "What else is there?"

Think about this: Have you ever been watching a movie, loving every second of it, but then, in the last 5 minutes, everything is ruined? You can hear people leaving the theater arguing about a bad ending. Nobody seems to argue about anything else. Even a fantastic party can be remembered as a terrible party if something bad happens in the last 5 minutes. The conclusion to your paper carries the same weight. People are passionate about endings. Don't disappoint your reader. Endings matter.

THREE CONCLUSIONS THAT DO MORE THAN SIMPLY REPEAT

Look at the word "formula." It suggests that there is shape or "form" to certain strategies. There is. I used to teach students how to give impromptu speeches. Once they thought of the speech as something that had a shape—something to pour information into—they felt comfortable. Think about your essay as having a shape. Most students already think of it as having a three-part shape—a beginning, middle, and end. Even though beginning writers seem to instinctively understand this—and they certainly recognize when an essay or a speech has no conclusion—they don't usually know what kind of material to pour into the end. While students feel like they can load almost any information into the body of the essay, conclusions leave them flummoxed. Let's start with the problem of repetition.

ZIP TIPS

Almost a No-Brainer

I know you have been told before to vary the length of your sentences, but you probably forget this simple (and easy) piece of advice when you are writing. Don't. Without really inventing an entirely new writing style and without really understanding the difference between a periodic sentence and a simple sentence, you can really predispose your reader to feeling that they are in good hands. Vary those sentences and reap the rewards.

Mirror Image of the Opening: Repeating with a Difference

Most college essays are relatively short. The ideas are not incredibly complicated and do not need to be reintroduced or even summarized. To repeat the ideas of the short essay on the fifth and final page is to insult your audience. It says, "I'm sure you can't remember what you just read 2 minutes ago."

Why not consider repeating the opening of your essay, but with a difference? If you began your essay with an anecdote, statistic, definition, question, or startling claim, then you should consider returning to that material, altering it slightly, and re-presenting it. This will not seem like empty repetition because you will not summarize so much as you will reinterpret, reimagine, or revisit the opening. It would be helpful to return to your anecdote, statistic, definition, question, or startling claim because your readers should now understand it in a different way, with new insight. You just need to show them the way.

Your conclusion might be considered a bookend to the introduction. Bookends hold several books together on a shelf; use this image of something that holds information together to further appreciate how introductions and conclusions work together. Note how the following two sentences serve to create a bookend form to our essay on television violence.

From the Introduction

> When most people think of violence, they imagine a fist, a knife, a gun, but not a word.

From the Conclusion

> *If most people think of violence exclusively as a physical phenomenon, something at the end of a fist, a knife, or a gun, it is all the more important that psychological and emotional violence, which is so often inflicted by a single word, be studied.*

The sentences cover much of the same ground, though the words have been changed enough for them to be different. They signal newly imagined, yet still familiar, material. It also suggests the larger significance of the essay's study. Our example, therefore, does not simply repeat. It addresses the significance of the essay's argument that a certain kind of violence (nonphysical or verbal violence) needs to be studied.

Mirror into the Future: Calls for Action

A call for action provides one of the most passionate endings, one that serves to inspire. The topic of violence lends itself to a passionate call to action, but so would a simple analysis of a short story. In the following two examples, you should note how the first example, an argumentative essay, begs for a call to action, while the second example, written for an analytical essay, also finds opportunities for a call to action.

> *Violence comes in many forms. Although most people continue to think of violence exclusively as a physical phenomenon, something at the end of a fist, a knife, or a gun, it can also be nonphysical. If we don't reprogram our*

minds to understand the very real threat of emotional and psychological violence, then we will continue to address only half of the problems facing our children. If we really want to have a profound effect on future generations, we must address the biased language that is tolerated in our

ZIP TIPS

How an Unsatisfying Conclusion Announces Itself

Imagine reading your essay in front of class. You deliver the final sentence and nothing happens, no applause. You look up at the startled faces. Your best friend has his hands ready to clap, but even he is unsure whether or not you've finished. The teacher is waiting. The whole class is waiting. Say something. Nobody likes silence. You sigh and nervously shuffle away from the podium. What should have been a climactic moment, full of satisfaction or simply relief, has instead fizzled.

You began your final sentence with the following words: *In conclusion*. How disappointing! Sure, people will recognize that it is time to applaud, but they will feel like you're begging for it. It is almost as if you are saying, "You can clap now." There are far more satisfying endings than the stiff and unimpressive "In conclusion" strategy.

school systems. We must translate the shocking findings of this research into real interventions and policies that will promote safe schools.

Toni Morrison's Beloved *offers one of the most devastating accounts of slavery and the legacy of slavery after emancipation. In beginning with the basic facts of Margaret Garner's real escape from slavery, Morrison cannot help but be aware of the burden of history as she creates fiction from fact. Just as this essay has tried to highlight the way the novel argues for its role as an alternative to history, so might future scholars begin to consider the biographical details of Morrison's life. How, for example, does her personal history or biography influence the questions she asks in the novel? How might our understanding of* Beloved *become richer with a more expansive consideration of Morrison's histories—both personal and communal?*

Beyond the Frame

What is the context for your argument? How does your topic relate to the larger world? How does your topic relate to very specific examples? What is just outside the frame of your study and how might it provide a final consideration of your essay's significance? Think of the many ways your essay may be compared to what remains just outside its frame. This conclusion may end with a generalization, a specific example, an analogy, or a question, but each serves the same function: to highlight significance by pointing beyond the frame of the essay.

The initiatives to create safe schools have a long history. Decades before the concept of safe schools existed, progressive educators fought to address inequities structured around race, gender, and even disability. If we really want to have a profound effect on future generations, we must address the biased language that still remains in our school systems. We must translate the shocking findings of the research into real interventions and policies that will promote safe schools. Just last year, William Penn High School became the first school in the state to introduce the safe school program. How long before other schools follow?

FINDING SIGNIFICANCE BY FREE-WRITING IN THE FIRST PERSON

You may feel uncomfortable writing first-person responses to a topic, but you do need to recognize that your conclusion cries out for personal reflection. Write it as a personal reflection, but then transform it into a more professional third-person exposition.

First-Person Narration Highlighting the Significance of the Essay

When I first came to the topic of violence on television, I was sure that it would be very easy. Then I began asking myself how I would define violence and should I include things like verbal abuse as violence. I was quite surprised by the research that connected verbal abuse with increases in suicide and physical assault. My proposal to introduce a safe school program to my old high school is no longer simply an empty classroom assignment. I am trying to save lives. My brother is a senior and my sister hasn't even started high school. I am trying to save real lives with names: Jason and Erin.

Transformed from First Person to a Professionally Objective Narration

When most people first come to the topic of violence on television, they imagine physical violence and not emotional or psychological violence. Many people, in fact, will resist labeling verbal abuse as violence. The research that connects verbal abuse with increases in suicide and physical assault needs to be disseminated. While parents and educators spend time worrying that their school might become a site for the next shootout or suicide, they really need to move from blaming violent media for every problem to understanding that schools foster a culture of abuse, a culture that not only allows students to verbally abuse one another, but frequently encourages it. In advocating the introduction of a safe school program at William Penn High School, this proposal does not simply seek to raise the consciousness of the administrators, educators, and students of that school. This proposal seeks to save lives.

DON'T BE ANXIOUS, BE CONFIDENT

If you have anxiety about writing a conclusion, get rid of it. While the word "conclusion" in your essay can signal an anxiety about concluding, a confident conclusion can make a big difference in the overall effect the essay has on the reader. Everything from sentence structure to word choice can convey this much-appreciated quality of assurance.

QUICK TIPS

- Don't raise a new topic, but do suggest the essay's larger significance. Feel free to leave the reader with a fresh image, a new insight, a consideration of the future, or a new piece of information.

- How can you introduce new information without raising a new topic? Sometimes students get confused about what is dangerously new, different, and out of place and what is merely a new way into the essay's main topic. A fresh image or a new insight, even a question that seems to point to the future and away from the present study, can be very relevant. In place of simple summary, give a question, insight, call to action, fresh image, detailed example, or broader context. Just make sure it relates to the essay.

- Don't repeat and don't summarize, but do provide a mirror image or a bookend.

- Recognize that the mirroring of the opening need not be a direct repetition. Get creative in making reference to the opening, but do not provide a conclusion that provides simple summary and dully repeated phrases, as if the reader has no memory.

- Don't use the word "conclusion" or "in summary" in letting your audience know that you are ending.

- There are so many ways to signal the end, strategies that provide stimulating new ways to add significance, meaning, and emotional depth to your argument or analysis. Find models in this chapter or in essays that you read for class. If a favorite essay ends with a question or quote, consider why it works in that essay and consider whether or not you want to use it as a guide.

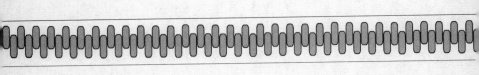

CHAPTER 9

The Exam Essay:
Easier Than You Think

THERE'S AN EXAM ESSAY FOR EVERYONE

Knowledge

Some exams simply serve to assess how much knowledge you retain. A wide range of questions may be employed to encourage you to write down all the information you remember. You can, however, transform this into an opportunity to evaluate or argue. For example, when asked for the characteristics of the Shakespearian and Petrarchan sonnets, many students will simply list the examples. But why not introduce a little argument or evaluation into your essay? You will probably find that it is easier to recall all

ZIP TIPS

You Can See into the Future

Examine the course description, goals, and assignments to predict what the exam essay will look like. Invent an essay question at the beginning of the semester. You can probably almost lift it from the syllabus. Place your essay question at the top of the syllabus and think about it at the beginning of each class. Every class lecture will then serve as a building block in creating that final essay.

the characteristics when your essay does more than simply list and, instead, argues or evaluates. A passive list of characteristics is transformed into an evaluation of the Shakespearian sonnet—more familiar and satisfying because it has many of the qualities of a play—dialogue and dramatization. This strategy, though it may seem like extra work, actually helps jog your memory for details or characteristics because you need them to evaluate one sonnet against the other.

Comprehension

Many essays serve to assess your comprehension of key terms and concepts. Consider whether the course has been designed around a complicated question of comprehension. For example, how do we comprehend educational practices or social structures? How do we discuss or debate the social construction of gender?

ZIP TIPS

Give 'Til It Hurts

Don't be afraid to give extra information. Not only will it add extra depth to your essay but it will also help you recall crucial information.

Application

Some courses show that the knowledge you have acquired needs to be applied to different situations. If you find that your teacher models the application of certain principles to new situations, you probably have been given fair warning that the essay exam will ask you to apply some of the ideas, strategies, concepts, and terms of the semester to a new subject or issue.

Analysis

Every discipline asks analytical questions. These exam essays will require you to consider patterns, systems, and relationships. The philosophy professor may ask you to analyze the ethics of a certain news story, perhaps even asking you to consider the ethics from different vantage points. The English professor may ask you to analyze a poem. Each of these tasks, of course, invites you to not only do more than analyze but also to show your knowledge of theorists or theoretical principles.

Evaluation

Evaluation, though not as common a feature of the essay exam as analysis, deserves our attention. Like each of the other categories, the evaluative essay also allows students to demonstrate their retention of knowledge and their comprehension of key principles. Evaluation, however, often allows the "weak" students to write very empty personal claims about the subject. Be careful to find support for your evaluative claims in facts and theories and not simply in personal reflection.

Argue

This essay type should make you feel confident because it will be very directed toward arguing a specific point. Remember to argue only one point. Too many essays are weakened by either sitting on the fence or hiding behind a wall. On the flip side, you must remember to address the opposition. Just be clear to present, and then address, points of opposition. You can address the opposition by either revealing weaknesses or flaws in their argument or by making a minor concession to their side, perhaps only to move on to a more important and compelling point for your side.

IT'S EXAM TIME! HELP!

Should I Spend Time Organizing My Thoughts?

Teachers recognize that the timed essay helps some students and hurts others, but they often believe it mostly helps the students who have done the readings and attended class. They often forget that it helps some students who are just faster—faster writers and faster thinkers. If I were given more than 40 minutes to write one essay, I would certainly devote 3 to 5 minutes gathering my ideas on an extra sheet of paper and even consider creating an outline. I would affix this "worksheet" to the very front of my submission.

I'm Drawing a Blank!

If you draw a blank, write down questions. Unlike the free-writing strategy that encourages you to state that you are stuck and then to consider why you are stuck, a list of questions will not look like you are unprepared. A list of questions, even when left unanswered, displays an inquiring mind.

If, for instance, you were asked to write an analysis of an advertisement (making use of some principles studied in your communications course), you might begin by asking questions. I suspect you could write a paragraph of questions and impress your teacher. Be confident that a more classically developed paragraph will follow. You may choose to label the list of questions as a worksheet or you may choose to actually begin with this creative list of questions.

ZIP TIPS
Distinguish Your Essay as Exemplary

- Go into the exam with at least one quote memorized. If you can't find a logical place for it in the body of the essay, then use it as an epigraph.

- Make sure you give your essay a title. Make sure it's a creative title, one that will surprise your professor.

- Highlight the significance of your various claims. Be free with those words that suggest emphasis: "most important part," "especially significant," and "perhaps most surprising." Show some personality.

Forgotten Names and Terms

You can't remember a name of a character, author, event, product, or theoretical term. Make up a substitute. If you remember it later, then feel free to erase the made-up term and insert the real term. Some of these made-up terms don't need to be corrected because they are already accurate. If you can't remember that Toni Morrison is the author of *Beloved*, refer to her as the "author of *Beloved*" and don't waste time straining yourself. If you remember that the author won the Nobel Prize refer to her as "the Nobel Prize winner," a strategy of substitution that solves the problem of ignorance by actually providing extra information, effectively winning points with your teacher. If you are trying to remember Maslow's hierarchy of needs, take what you've got and run with it: Call it "Maslow's theory" or "the system of prioritizing needs." The last example may seem awkward, but it is better to show your knowledge of the general principle than to lose precious time. This is not a game show; this is an essay.

Nothing Left to Say?

What should you do if there is lots of time left, but you feel as if you have nothing left to say? Don't leave early. Your professor will remember that you left early, and, unless your exam is brilliant, your early escape will seem to suggest a paucity of ideas or perhaps an unwillingness to take the exam seriously. How do you continue to write without repeating yourself?

Insert More Context

Consider whether your essay needs more context for your discussion, analysis, or argument. Perhaps your essay could benefit from a detailed definition of a complex term, some historical background that sets up the key issue or question, or a developed address to the resisting reader. The new paragraph will probably be best inserted as your second paragraph, and you can easily add transitions into the preexisting body of the essay.

Insert More Significance

Remember the idea of adding significance to your analysis, argument, or discussion? It would not be difficult to add significance in a single paragraph. In fact, essay exams are frequently devoid of this type of commentary. Consider adding a paragraph at the end that goes over each aspect (each paragraph) of the essay, reflecting on the significance of each contribution.

TIME'S UP ALREADY!?!?!

Will This Exam Essay Be Read as Carefully as My Other Essays?

Every essay is read with a different set of criteria, but your professors will certainly recognize that they should not expect the same content (quotations, research, detailed examples) or care (tight organization, developed paragraphs, spelling accuracy) in an essay exam. Don't take this as permission to write drivel. In fact, I would suggest that you try to distinguish yourself by indeed including some of those features that your professor will not expect to see.

Will My Teacher Read This Essay with an Open Mind?

Exam essays often get read at the end of a long and tiring semester, after your professor has already gotten to know you. Some professors may be guilty of skimming your paper for key pieces of information. Do not give your teacher any chance to miss your brilliance. In addition to beginning with a powerful title and a thought-provoking epigraph, begin the essay with a surprisingly important observation. Spend extra time creating a strong, and perhaps thought-provoking, introduction. If the prompt or question for the exam essay seems to invite you to cover some ground, feel free to highlight the crucial parts of your essay. Consider underlining key sections or dividing the essay with subheadings. It will be difficult for the professor to miss these highlighted points.

My Teacher Will Be Impressed by How Many Pages I Write, Right?

A paper that has extra words in the form of repetitions, digressions, and even loose language will receive lower marks than a shorter paper that covers the same ground. Think of your essay like a movie. If you watch a movie that drags in the middle or takes too long to finish, you think less of it. Don't let your essay drag!

FIVE TRICKS TO WRITING THE EXAM ESSAY

1. Don't introduce anything. There is no time. Just throw yourself into the essay by placing your thesis statement, question, or claim in the very first sentence.

2. Even if you don't begin by creating an outline, you should take a few moments to imagine sections of your essay. Be sure that you create topic sentences

for each section. The topic sentence is more important in this timed essay than in any other essay.

3. Although you may instinctively understand that you should load the essay with terms, facts, and concepts from class lectures and readings, be sure to demonstrate your comprehension of those terms, facts, and concepts by defining and evaluating them.

4. Provide an interesting title and epigraph. This should take very little time and it will make your essay look like a careful and considered work of art.

5. Save time to write a conclusion. If possible, use a quote or other detail that reinforces your ability to reflect upon this concrete detail. Don't forget to answer why this specific detail serves as an opportunity to reflect on the larger concerns, questions, or issues addressed in your essay. If you run out of time, provide at least one sentence to create closure, perhaps simply stating how the last thought relates to the overarching issue presented in your introduction or thesis.

CHAPTER 10

Scary Thoughts on Plagiarism and Research

RESEARCH IS NOW easier than ever. You can quickly find online full-text articles, dictionaries, encyclopedias, and even primary texts, such as novels and biographies. If you don't understand plagiarism, you may actually hurt your paper rather than improve it. If you don't understand how the rise in plagiarism has affected how teachers grade, then you may be at a disadvantage.

IS IT EASY TO CATCH PLAGIARISM?

Plagiarism is now easier than ever. Catching plagiarism is also now easier than ever.

Teachers have a number of tricks for catching plagiarism. There are services that allow professors to run papers or parts of papers through special search engines. If you think you can buy a great essay, remember you may be buying your way into plagiarism, a failing grade, and even academic probation (if not worse).

One semester, I had students submit four papers anonymously. The papers were graded and only later did the students attach their names. By the third assignment, I was able to recognize many of the papers as belonging to specific students. In fact, I was so confident that I returned several anonymous papers to the right students, the whole class watching in awe as if I had performed a magic trick. If it's possible to recognize so much in a short time, your teacher can certainly recognize when a radically different prose style or mastery of language gets plunked down into your paper. Don't plagiarize.

HOW PLAGIARISM CAN AFFECT YOUR GRADE

Because plagiarism is such a widespread problem, professors read papers with an eye of suspicion. Just one superbly wrought sentence or masterfully placed theoretical term can make your teacher suspicious, especially if it seems out of place for your writing.

If a professor feels material has been plagiarized but is unable to find enough evidence to confront the student, the essay is still under suspicion. A writer never wants his or her reader to feel unsure about the originality of the work. It is, therefore, crucial that you take care in presenting materials that are not only original but also seem original. Don't write a paper that even looks plagiarized.

How to Ensure Your Work Seems Original and Not Plagiarized

- Don't use words that you don't understand. Some students think they will impress their teachers by using sophisticated concepts, but if you don't fully understand those concepts, it will seem as if you are just cutting and pasting a few phrases, ideas, or even sentences without fully recognizing what you are doing.

- Don't use quotations as a crutch. It is better to use only quotations that you fully understand and can fully incorporate and respond to in your own words.

- Most important, when you use someone else's words or ideas, consider how to distinguish your contribution from their ideas.

USING (AND NOT BEING USED BY) RESEARCH

You've worked hard and you want credit for doing your research. But if you simply gather information into an essay, you may prove your research skills but not your ability to synthesize, analyze, and argue. Don't let the research serve as a substitute for what the assignment really asks of you. Don't let your voice disappear or opinions sit in the shadow. Don't let your creative and analytical ideas fizzle out before the great brilliance of the published professionals you so respectfully quote. Here are some surprisingly easy solutions to holding your own with the masters.

Question Authority

You have been schooled in absorbing the ideas, words, and facts presented by others. Stop it. Interrupt that pattern of respectful absorption of other people's ideas. The easiest way to highlight your contribution to your research paper is to challenge the ideas of a published author. Get in the habit of reading as a doubter. To prepare students for the essay, I often have them write a critique of a published essay. It is very liberating for them to challenge ideas and many of these essays get used to build their larger essay.

Build upon the Work of Others

Although challenging a published author is a good way to distinguish your contribution, many students find it difficult to find something to challenge. It is, however, easy to find published ideas that invite opportunities for analysis, questioning, research, or interpretation. The second easiest way to distinguish your contribution is to present the idea of a published author and then explore how that idea can be extended, revised, complicated, continued down a different path, applied to something else, or considered in a different light.

Synthesize Ideas

If one article presents information about the effects of watching violent images on television and another article presents information about the receptivity of children raised in authoritarian households, you might wonder if the two studies might be combined (or synthesized) into an argument about the especially profound effect of violent images on a specific group of people. This example of synthesizing materials creates something new because the first article says nothing about authoritarian households and the second article says nothing about violent images. You have made certain connections that are totally unique. Challenge yourself to bring very different research together and seek to find the connections—and then highlight them.

WHAT TO RESEARCH FOR THE NONRESEARCH PAPER

Author or Key Figure

Whether you are writing about a novel, a historical event, or a controversial subject, there is a key figure or "author" of that text or event. While your professor may have already presented some information about the first woman senator or the author of a novel, it could be very useful to have even more information. This new information can distinguish your paper from the other essays.

Complex Idea or Term

The complex idea or term may be a central concern of the course and so many students will wonder why they should gather even more information on it. A quick Internet search may not only provide a contrasting opinion, definition, or view of the complex idea or term, but may offer different language or examples that help you to further understand its complexity. In introducing other viewpoints or even other voices, your essay gathers strength.

Examples and Illustrations

If every other essay builds its support with the same selection of examples and illustrations, which students gather from course readings or lectures, your essay, which will provide a fresh example or illustration, will surely capture your professor's interest.

Online Resources

Some wonderful resources are available online. Many college libraries have databases that provide complete articles that are identical to the journal articles used in scholarly research. Be sure to cite these sources.

If you are using a Web site to help clarify your ideas, be careful not to plagiarize. Discuss these issues with your professor. You will only gain more of his or her respect as you describe your extra work, your sincerity in distinguishing your ideas from those of another, and your concern with not plagiarizing.

Many online resources are developed with little review and will mark your essay as unprofessional if you choose to quote them. Do not quote from online resources like Wikipedia, personal Web sites (even if they belong to scholars), or commercial sites (marked with ".com" in the URL). These online resources, however, may lead you to more traditional resources via bibliographies or the mention of a crucial article or book.

CHAPTER 11

You're Minutes Away from a Great Revision

MOST STUDENTS BECOME deathly ill when teachers mention the word revision. If you are capable of actually reading a few words about revision, you may have what it takes to write a paper far superior to every other student paper. Why? The real trick to writing is in the revising. Let's try to make it as painless as possible.

LET ME COUNT THE WAYS

The 60-Second Artsy Revision

Spread your paper across the table. Don't read a single word; just look at it. Examine the pages as if they are works of art. What do you see? In less than a minute, you should begin to find some problems. Common errors that are easily seen when you view the pages as works of art include:

- Missing indents at the beginning of paragraphs

- Questionable lengths for paragraphs perhaps indicating some paragraphs that need development or others that need to be split into two

- A lack of italicized words or quotation marks, which may indicate that you forgot to format book titles or place the titles of smaller works, such as articles and poems, in quotation marks

The 5-Minute Revision for Glaring Mistakes

Read your essay out loud. Listen for problems with the prose or even the logic. Make sure that you have a pencil in hand to write down the problems that are easiest to discover, which will usually fall into the following categories:

- Missing words

- Awkward phrases

- Repetitive word choice or sentence structure

- Questionable grammar or spelling

Don't slow down to write comments about larger issues of logic or argument, but instead draw an arrow in the margin to remind you to revisit that section of the paper.

This trick works even better if you have someone else read the essay aloud while you underline and take notes on a separate copy. If you don't have help, tape record yourself reading the essay, play it back, and take notes on the problems that you now can hear.

The 10-Minute Guide to Revising the Important Words

Circle every verb. If every other verb is "is," then you need to work on activating your verbs.

Underline every sentence's subject. If every sentence seems to place the subject at the beginning of the sentence, rethink your sentence structure. If the same subject, without variation, gets repeated over and over, consider synonyms or substitute structures. You may also choose to refer to your subject in oblique ways, such as calling it "this problem," "our study," or simply "this."

The 10-Minute Guide to Revising Your Common Mistakes

Gather your old papers together and examine their most common mistakes. Make a list of the five most common errors. If you were to spend no more than 2 minutes on each error, you would spend a total of 10 minutes correcting these five most common errors. Learn from your mistakes. If you frequently place quotation marks in the wrong place, spend 2 minutes examining your quotations. If you frequently misspell names, give a quick check. Even more complicated common errors, such as weak introductions or unsupported claims, can benefit from this quick and targeted review.

The 10-Minute Guide to Revising Everyone's Most Common Mistakes

The votes are in and every teacher agrees. The number one problem with student essays can be found in the thesis or in the lack of a thesis. Why do students think they have a thesis when they don't? Why do they think it is clear when it is not? How could they assume it had the right scope when it was too broad? How could they believe there was something to argue when there clearly was not? Try asking the following questions—as if the essay were not written by you:

- So what?

- Why should I care? What's interesting about this subject?

- Have you considered looking at this in a very different way?

- Is the author straddling the fence and unable to commit to one argument?

- Are there really two or three subjects here?

- Won't that take many, many pages to cover?

The first two questions consider the significance of the project. Is the topic worth considering or have you chosen something that everyone would already agree to without any debate or discussion? The middle two questions consider whether the thesis invites opposing views or debate and whether or not the essay takes a firm position. The final two questions, the most important questions to ask, consider the scope of the essay. Most student essays need to find a tighter focus.

The 30-Minute Guide to Revising Organization

After you have completed a first draft, write an outline for it. Let's call this a reverse outline. This reverse outline helps those writers who feel most comfortable generating ideas through writing and not outlining. The reverse outline can indicate whether there is a logical structure to the essay and whether the paragraphs do indeed contain relevant information.

HE OR SHE EQUALS THEY

The Student Government president comes to your class and asks everyone to sign a petition to have February 19th declared a

National Day of Remembrance for those sent to Japanese internment camps during World War II. You've read about this shameful part of our history and you are sympathetic with this consciousness-raising event. You read the petition. You are ready to sign. Then you notice the final two sentences: "We believe every student should make an impassioned plea to each of his professors

ZIP TIPS

Social Sciences, History, Political Science, and Business Essays Just Aren't Creative Fodder, Right?

You have to be creative, but also recognize what works. Most professors—even those associated with the arts—will not appreciate an essay that veers from the assignment. They will not be entranced with an essay that decides to become poetry in the middle of its argument or has a reference to *The Simpsons* that can hardly be connected to the main subject of the paper. Save the colored paper, the sparkles, the changing font size, and the wavy letters. But be creative in your use of language. One of the easiest ways to show a creative flair is by examining your verbs. Let me rewrite the last sentence to "show" you what I mean: "Invigorate your verbs and dazzle your reader."

for their support. In fact, we also ask that you write the governor to demand that he declare February 19th a National Day of Remembrance."

What is the problem with this petition? The most startling part of the petition refers to the governor as a "he" but your governor is a woman. You begin to look at the other pronouns and find more problems. The first problem suggests that the writers don't know that there is a female governor (a failure of knowledge), while the other problems can be classified as problems with grammar and imagination. A document that seeks to convince and influence readers cannot afford to make such blunders.

Let's take a closer look at the first sentence:

> *We believe every student should make an impassioned plea to each of his professors for their support.*

Although the masculine singular pronoun (he, him, his) has historically served as a generic pronoun, capable of referring to both sexes, this is quickly changing. Interestingly, writing inclusively is not that difficult, which makes this problematic first sentence even more serious. Let's examine two problems with the sentence. Some students may find the petition's reference to "his professors" sexist and noninclusive. This is especially unfortunate in a petition that seeks to advance understanding of different identities. In addition to this problem, the last part of the sentence makes use of a plural pronoun ("their") although it refers back to the singular pronoun "each." It is grammatically incorrect.

There are many solutions to these problems, everything from unsightly inventions like "s/he" to cumbersome references to "he or she." However, if you simply transform singular nouns into the plural, you can solve most problems with great ease.

every student should ask his professor → students should ask their professors

if a politician asks for your vote, tell him → if politicians ask for your vote, tell them

COMMON MISTAKES THAT ARE DIFFICULT TO FORGIVE BUT EASY TO CORRECT

Poor Grammar

Your professors, regardless of their discipline, will take note of your grammar usage as a basic sign of your intelligence, past preparation, and future possibilities. Even if a professor's grading rubric suggests that grammar is not extremely important, it will be a factor in that professor's evaluation of the overall intellect of the essay.

No Title

Get in the habit of writing a title for everything, even an in-class exam essay.

Misspelled Names

Students always misspell names, even the names of their professors (is that a way to help your grade?) and the names of key authors discussed in the essay (making it hard to claim authority over the subject).

Homonyms

Three homonyms get misspelled frequently: their/there, its/it's, and to/too/two. I'm sympathetic to these mistakes because I have a brain that processes sound more than image, but these simple mistakes will make some teachers place you in the category of slow-witted.

Words Missing/Repeated

Your word-processing program should place a noticeable mark under the offending problem, so there is little excuse for missing or repeated words.

Improper Form for Book Titles/Articles

A large text, like the novel *Beloved*, should be placed in italics, but a smaller text, like an article called "Unusual Themes in Toni Morrison's *Beloved*," should be placed in quotation marks.

CHAPTER 12

Flirting with the Future

HOW ARE YOUR CLASSES ALL RELATED?

Students tend to think of each essay as an isolated task or each type of class as unrelated to the next. Instead, think of your college career as one continuous exercise in building your thinking and communication skills. When you keep this in mind, you will want to make connections between your experiences in each class. How can Introduction to Psychology help you perform better in American Literature and how can American Literature help you in Philosophy? It is not just the content that should be carried from class to class but the skills in analysis and writing.

AND WHAT DOES THIS HAVE TO DO WITH THE REAL WORLD?

Soon you will be out of school and in a profession. Soon you will have to set your own goals, serve as your own critic, and learn without as much guidance. Why not discover in college how to become your own best coach and advocate? Begin to think of every class as moving you closer to the skill set that you need. If a class challenges your patience, be a problem solver and figure out how to make it more rewarding, more entertaining, more interesting. If you can't challenge yourself to find the best in your college experience, you should not expect everything to change when you enter the "real" world.

LEARNING FROM YOUR ESSAYS

It should be especially easy to consciously learn from your past writings because you receive documents, the graded essays, which should be gathered together into a portfolio of work. Save everything. You can learn from examining these documents over the years.

Make a hit list of your biggest problems. This helps writers focus on the task at hand. While writing the next paper, and especially during the editing phase, this list of both large and small issues should be addressed. If you repeatedly construct disorganized, digressive, and gigantic papers, is it a problem with your thesis? Do you need to focus more? If you tend to have weak introductions, spend extra time on introductions. If your last paper received strong marks, but the comments suggest areas for improvement, such as a need to "provide more support" or "better organization," take these as constructive criticism and try to correct the problems.

WHY GOOD WRITERS ARE AT A DISADVANTAGE

Professors, who often need to grade many papers, tend to write fewer comments on the strong papers. If you already have skills, your solid grades may keep you from getting the necessary feedback to help you be the best that you can be. If you hope to make a career in writing or if you hope to go to graduate school, you should be especially nervous about receiving only praise. How will you learn how to improve so that you can compete against other outstanding writers?

After Your Next A+ Paper

After receiving an A+ paper with very few comments, tell your professor that you want to improve your writing. Ask for extra feedback. Your professor will be sympathetic and impressed. You may even get a private tutorial and build a friendship with a mentor who may write you letters of recommendation. Don't be shy. Your future depends on your ability to push yourself.

GETTING FEEDBACK

Don't think of your professor as a judgmental authority figure but as helpful guide. Here are some helpful hints on visiting your professor after receiving a disappointing grade:

- Do not go immediately after receiving the graded paper; give yourself time to process the comments, the grade, and your emotions.

- Let your professor know that you are not challenging the grade, but that you want to learn how to write better.

- Do not ask what aspect of the paper cost you the most points, which suggests that you are only interested in the grade; instead ask what aspect of the paper needs the most work.

- Ask if the professor will look at the beginning stages, thesis, or first paragraph of your next paper.

FIVE FANTASTIC REASONS FOR SAVING ALL YOUR ESSAYS

1. These are the documents of your college career!

2. As time passes, you will read these documents in different ways. You may understand them better. If you feel that a teacher is an unfair grader, it will be interesting to look at the paper a year later to see if you still believe that to be true.

3. You may be asked to write on a similar subject later, you may wonder where a certain quote came from, or you may want to use an old paper to kick-start ideas for a new paper.

4. You may apply to graduate school and it would be nice to refer back to relevant papers (such as arguing in your application essay for law school that you wrote three papers as an undergraduate that had to do with ethics and the law). Maybe that application essay can refer to the titles of those essays or even quote what a teacher stated on one of those essays.

5. Chances are you will learn and grow during your four years at college, but you won't know how much you have learned and grown unless you save these documents from your early years. Do yourself a favor, save these documents so that you can see how you continue to grow and evolve as a writer and thinker.

WHAT TO DO WITH THE PERFECT ESSAY YOU'VE WRITTEN

- Search the Web for publishing outlets and awards for undergraduate work. There are actually many, some local and some national, and they change from year to year. Meet with your professor and discuss what you have found, providing a list of names or guidelines. Ask for advice. Ask also whether your professor knows of other journals to which you might submit your essay for publication.

- Ask your teacher if you can further your study in this area, perhaps by building an independent study around the paper with the intention of developing it into either a senior thesis or just a more advanced paper, one that might be submitted to appropriate journals.

- Consider how the ideas for this one paper could be connected with the concerns of another discipline. Meet with a favorite professor in that other discipline and discuss whether the paper might lead to a different but related project. Explain that you are not trying to recycle work but rather develop into a deep and sophisticated thinker.

- Some of this advice encourages you to think about developing or publishing your essay. This is especially appropriate for students who may apply to graduate school (the writing sample is a crucial part of the application) or who may soon be in the job market. Because this is your best essay, I suggest that you document the experience by writing a short narrative about the development of your idea, some of the things you learned in writing the paper, and perhaps its strongest aspects. Save this narrative for when you really need to promote yourself in a job interview or on a graduate school application. Be very articulate about this essay's strengths and its genesis—after all, it's your best one! Congratulations!

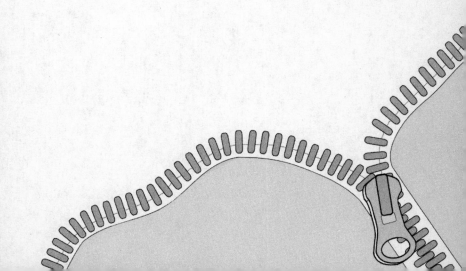

EPILOGUE

From Myth to Reality

THE DANGER OF MYTHS

Writing manuals tend to produce myths, especially about what you should never do. Be suspicious of any rules that might strip writing of its mystery, artistry, or vitality. If I have slipped up from time to time, rip the offending page from this book. If you feel this book encourages you to conform or abandon your creativity for formula, throw the entire book into the trash bin.

Recognize that some conventions, such as using "I" in a sentence, are acceptable in some disciplines and totally unacceptable in others. Some aspects of form, such as where to place quotation marks, are different in England and Canada. Some stylistic features, such as the complexity of sentences, have changed over the years. And some rules of style, such as whether to begin a sentence with a conjunction like "and," are quickly changing because popular styles are increasingly influencing academic styles. Language is alive and always changing.

All of these differences in "the rules," which can be traced to different writing communities, should be cause to celebrate the great elasticity of language. Let's examine some of the most common myths, which primarily strip writing and the college experience of complexity. It is important to embrace and not resist complexity. You will learn much faster.

Myth: The teacher has a single answer in mind.

Reality: Most higher-level assignments do not invite a single "correct" answer. Even if a teacher can imagine a specific solution to the assignment, most will stay open to different solutions and even give contrary interpretations high grades when the essay provides a strong argument with great support. Even math professors, when grading a proof that arrives at the wrong answer, will examine the path toward that solution.

Myth: Open assignments are easier to write than closed or defined topics.

Reality: Imagine one assignment that requires you to write a story based on the Mona Lisa and a second assignment that invites you to walk into the Louvre to find the perfect painting to build a story around. You are going to lose a lot of time in the second assignment and you are going to always wonder if there is a better painting to choose.

Myth: Don't raise questions in your essay unless you can answer them.

Reality: Published authors always raise impossible-to-answer questions. A good question (even when it is impossible to answer) demonstrates a writer's analytical talents as much as an interesting claim. Don't feel like every question needs to be answered. Some questions should simply suggest the reach of your imagination.

Myth: Make your essay look unique.

Reality: The content, and not the font, should stand out. The quality of the prose, and not the quality or color of the paper, should stand out. When a paper offers visual extras (increased font size, wavy letters, colored paper or ink, or exotic paper clips or binders), it suggests that it has little of substance to offer and it will be juvenile, rather than professional.

Myth: Your thesis should appear at the end of the first paragraph.

Reality: Every formula for writing is a fiction that serves to reduce writing down to a few choices. The specific project, however, should determine which choice to make. Longer essays (12–25 pages) may logically need longer introductions and the thesis may best appear in the second or third paragraph. Controversial subjects may invite an unfolding thesis and the clearest claim may not come until the end of the essay. Most essays written for college are relatively short (3–10 pages) and logic will most probably dictate that the thesis appear in the classic slot at the end of the first paragraph. When writing short essays (1–2 page position papers) or essays for exams, consider placing your thesis in the very first line. Remember, even though I have provided a few more formulas, they are still just formulas, waiting for a unique situation to invite other solutions.

Myth: Your introduction should state what the essay will cover, just as the conclusion will state what the essay has just stated.

Reality: To make writers feel more comfortable, someone invented the logic that the introduction "tells you what WILL BE SAID, the body of the essay then STATES IT, and the conclusion tells you WHAT HAS JUST BEEN SAID." This simplistic formula has gotten many students into trouble. If your introduction or conclusion lends itself to repetition, the essay will seem weak. An introduction, for example, can use many more strategies (anecdote, authoritative quote, or contemporary event) to introduce the subject. A conclusion has just as many possibilities and should not simply restate what has just been stated. If the beginning and ending of any document must argue for its worth, don't throw the opportunity away on repetition.

Myth: You should not bring up a new topic in the conclusion.

Reality: Yes and no. What topic do you want to raise? How are you asking us to think about that "new" topic? If you have written an essay that argues that reality TV has become more popular because people no longer feel a sense of community, then you certainly might see a connection between this and the rise of Web communities. This is a phenomenon that might also be explained by looking at changing social structures. Should you mention this in a conclusion? A distracting mention of this related topic might appear in the following manner:

> *"Computers have also allowed communities to build, and these new Web-based communities are more popular than ever."*

Anywhere in the essay, but especially in the conclusion, this new subject will seem like a digression. If you feel it is important to mention this new topic, highlight its connection to the main topic. Try:

> *"If reality TV fills a need for a fractured society, it is certainly not the only cultural phenomena to do so. Future research might examine the explosion of Web communities as also*

responsive to the needs of our disconnected society. Reality TV, however, provides the most fascinating response because it provides little more than an illusion of connection."

Note how this example works to keep the new subject always related and in the service of the larger topic. If this seems too difficult to manage, do not introduce that new subject no matter how tempting it seems.

Myth: A paragraph should have four or five sentences.

Reality: Don't count. Instead, consider what information develops the topic sentence. Don't count. Instead, examine the organic nature of the paragraph, which should feel whole, coherent, and proportioned.

Myth: In writing the essay exam, you should focus on quantity.

Reality: If you focus too much on QUANTITY, you may haphazardly dive into the essay, rambling your way through ideas and frontloading the essay with filler. On the other hand, if you are too focused on QUALITY, you may spend too much time thinking and organizing your thoughts and not enough time writing. I think most students can benefit from a few minutes of preparation, which hopefully results in a framework for organization where three key points can be made.

Myth: It is important to have only the most current research.

Reality: Some writers mistakenly believe newer is better. It is not necessarily so. Look at recently published articles and books. Do they refer to older articles and books? Are there some older publications that everyone refers to? There are real advantages to including research—no matter the topic—that is very current. If the publications are extremely recent, you are proving that the essay is not plagiarized. Young writers, however, often reveal their ignorance of the discipline by ignoring older publications that published authors are still using. Remember, professionals have already published articles with extensive bibliographies. Study those bibliographies and then build from there.

Myth: In revising, I should work with other students only if they are better writers.

Reality: Weak writers may not be able to correct your grammar or paragraph structure, but they can certainly tell you what they don't understand or when they became confused. If a weak writer simply read through the paper and placed a check alongside the confusing passages, you would have been given a great gift—not the solution but an indication of the problem.

Myth: There are good writers and bad writers.

Reality: There is good writing and bad writing, but writers are made and not born. There is a saying that if you want to become a good writer you should write. Is it that simple? Yes, write and write a lot, but also learn to read like an editor or even a teacher. When my students become tutors in the writing lab, they evolve from good writers to great writers. In becoming good teachers or tutors, they become good students of the English language. There are no bad or hopeless writers; just writers who could use a few tricks.

NOTES UNZIPPED

NOTES UNZIPPED

NOTES UNZIPPED

NOTES UNZIPPED

NOTES UNZIPPED

NOTES UNZIPPED

NOTES UNZIPPED

NOTES UNZIPPED

NOTES UNZIPPED

NOTES UNZIPPED

GIVE US YOUR FEEDBACK

Peterson's, a Nelnet company, publishes a full line of resources to help guide you through the college admission process. Peterson's publications can be found at your local bookstore, library, and high school guidance office, and you can access us online at www.petersons.com.

We welcome any comments or suggestions you may have about this publication and invite you to complete our online survey at www.petersons.com/booksurvey. Or you can fill out the paper survey on the next page, tear it out, and mail it to us at:

Publishing Department
Peterson's
2000 Lenox Drive
Lawrenceville, NJ 08648